CANOEING THE BOUNDARY WATERS WILDERNESS

A SAWBILL LOG

STEPHEN WILBERS

THE History PRESS

Published by The History Press
Charleston, SC 29403
www.historypress.net

Cover images: The author's favorite campsite on his favorite lake: "A calm surface with mirrored clouds"; lower photos from left: the autho's wife on Sawbill Lake, a favorite Hazel Lake campsite, the author and his son wading the stream leading from Hazel Lake.

Part of chapter two, "In Search of a Whole, Live Moose," was published previously in the *Northern Review* 2, no. 1 (Spring 1988) by the University of Wisconsin-Stevens Point Foundation Press, Inc.

Excerpts from the documentary film *The Wilderness World of Sigurd F. Olson*, distributed by the Listening Point Foundation, Inc., listeningpointfoundation.org. Copyright 1980. Reprinted with permission from Ray Christensen.

Jan Zita Grover, excerpts from *In Northern Waters*. Copyright 1979 by Jan Zita Grover. Reprinted with the permission of The Permissions Company, Inc., on behalf of Graywolf Press, Minneapolis, Minnesota, www.graywolfpress.org.

Paul Gruchow, excerpts from *Boundary Waters: The Grace of the Wild* (Minneapolis, MN: Milkweed Editions, 1997). Copyright 1977 by Paul Gruchow. Reprinted with permission from Milkweed Editions, www.milkweed.org.

First published 2012

Manufactured in the United States

ISBN 978.1.60949.732.3

Library of Congress CIP data applied for.

Notice: The information in this book is true and complete to the best of our knowledge. It is offered without guarantee on the part of the author or The History Press. The author and The History Press disclaim all liability in connection with the use of this book.

This is a deeply personal, yet universal story. Stephen Wilbers keenly observes nature, within the wilderness and within the human heart. A well-told memoir that is funny, poignant and ultimately profound.

—Bill Hansen
Sawbill Canoe Outfitters

Stephen Wilbers has a deep knowledge of the lakes, rivers and portages of the Boundary Waters, as well as the rich legacy of literature that the wilderness boasts. He has new and interesting things to say about the canoe country, but he does not try to repeat the thoughts of the many great writers who have come before him. Wilbers carefully weaves quotes and excerpts from his predecessors into his own fine stories about his travels by paddle.

—Greg Seitz
Friends of the Boundary Waters Wilderness

Sure, Stephen Wilbers takes us paddling into the solitude and ethereal stillness of the Boundary Waters Canoe Area Wilderness. We quake to the haunting calls of loons and wolves, gape at the shimmering curtains of the northern lights, look expectantly for the iconic moose. But the richest and most engaging qualities of Wilbers's memoir are its social scenes. Far from being alone in the wilderness, he is surrounded by family and friends. His canoe trips are touchstones to the people he loves. It is a rich look at not only nature, but also humanity.

—Greg Breining
Author of *Paddle North: Canoeing the Boundary Waters–Quetico Wilderness*

Stephen Wilbers invites you to canoe with him "to a place that grabbed a part of [his] heart and never let go." Through his captivating descriptions you will hear the silence of the wilderness, paddle through the fragrant water lilies searching for the elusive, full-antlered bull moose and sleep under a blanket of stars beyond your imagination. You will even learn the secret to the age-old question every fisherman wants to know: "Is this lake good for fishing?" His seven-year-old son Eddy knows the answer.

—Betty Vos Hemstad
Author of *Wildflowers of the Boundary Waters: Hiking through the Seasons*

In these pages that carry us deep into the Boundary Lakes wilderness, Stephen Wilbers tells us that "you have to let it become part of who you are." Discover here, then, writing that's an outcome of that merging, fine writing, pure and true as the silent glide of a canoe across shining waters in the still of evening. Discover here, as well, a story of love for family and friends and those bewitching wilderness lakes that, over the decades, Wilbers has come to know so very well. And discover, too, within this complexly beautiful volume, a bit of that eternity from which we've risen but so seldom glimpse in our daily lives.

—JOE PADDOCK
Author of *Keeper of the Wild: The Life of Ernest Oberholtzer*

Through Stephen Wilbers's eyes and pen, we once again experience the Boundary Waters Canoe Area Wilderness and come to know its points, rocks, portages and the very trees themselves. What a wealth we are given as we benefit not only from Wilbers's memory but his own vast inner library of quotes, perfectly placed, from the likes of Paul Gruchow, Doug Wood, Bud Heinselman, Greg Breining, Florence Page Jaques or Ernest Oberholtzer, and of course Sig Olson. Yet to me, this second volume from Wilbers's logbook takes on true form and meaning because of Eddy, the author's son, whom we watch grow from age four (baby toads in the water jugs) to a tall twenty-two who makes the wilderness his own at every turn. It is through Eddy that we feel the movement of time, through his humor and antics that we love our own children even more.

—BETH WATERHOUSE
Executive Director, the Ernest Oberholtzer Foundation

To Debbie, who loves wilderness but doesn't care for bears on the campsite.

To Eddy, who helped me rediscover the mystery of nature.

To Kate and Markus, who make canoeing fun.

And to Dad, who was my loyal companion for all those years.

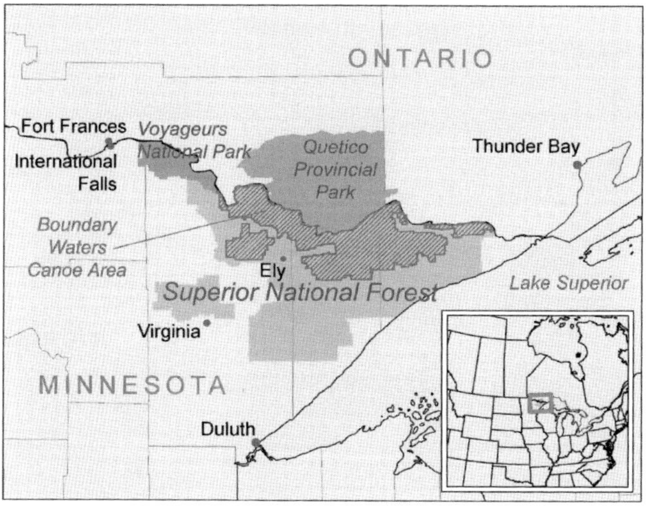

Map of the Boundary Waters Canoe Area Wilderness in northeastern Minnesota. *This file is licensed under the Creative Commons Attribution-Share Alike 3.0 Unported license.*

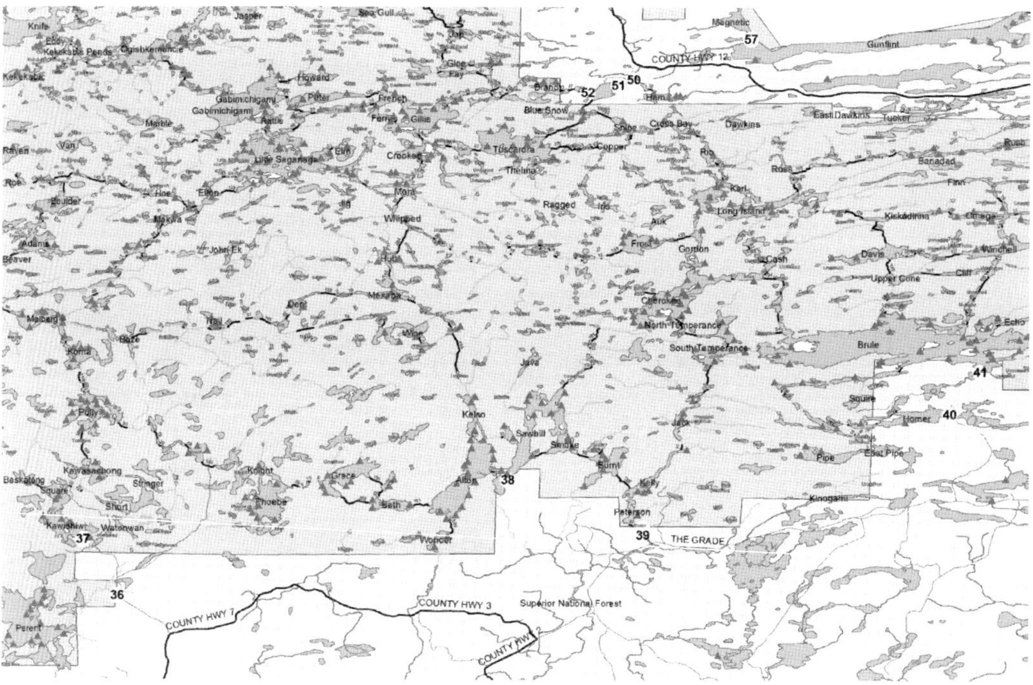

Boundary Waters wilderness lakes and campsites, depicting entry point 38 (Sawbill Lake) and Hazel Lake (west of Phoebe and Knight). *Reprinted with permission from Adam Amato of bwca.com.*

Contents

Contents

ACKNOWLEDGEMENTS

Although my trips with them are not part of this story, I want to thank the members of my men's group for being such good and faithful friends. They're an important part of my life. I also want to thank William Burleson, Megan Marsnik and Jeanne Ritterson for their encouraging words and critical comments. I've been meeting with these talented writers monthly ever since I took Mary Gardner's novel-writing class at the Loft Literary Center in the winter of 2009–10. Fortunately for me, our writers' group evolved from offering critiques of short excerpts to reading book-length manuscripts just as I was completing this one. I am indebted to them for their insights and suggestions.

Whenever I saw him for the past several years, my friend Joe Paddock would ask me how my "Boundary Waters book" was coming. I first met Joe in the late 1980s, when I was working as the associate director of the University of Minnesota's creative writing program, but I really got to know him at a series of writers' retreats on Mallard Island, where preservationist Ernest Oberholtzer lived for fifty years and whose biography Joe has written. I thank Joe for his faith in my abilities, his friendship and his unfailing interest in my "Boundary Waters book," now two books.

I also want to recognize Tom and Barb Balcom, Don Maronde and Beth Waterhouse, Pam Joern, Scott King, Pam McClanahan, Ken Meter, Nancy Paddock, Janet Pearson, Jean Replinger and Connie Szarke—the other Mallard Island writers who took their chances with the creative process and who encouraged me in my own efforts.

Debbie, the guiding force in the author's life.

Finally, I want to thank my wife, Debbie, who understands my passions and mostly puts up with them. My passion for her is the guiding force in my life. I was sorry I had to cut her chapter, as well as chapters about canoeing with Eddy and Kate, from my first Boundary Waters book to stay within the 150-page limit stipulated in my book contract. "There was so much love for our children in those chapters," she said. "They should have been part of your book." I hope with this book to make up for those omissions.

Introduction

Before You Embark

You're about to set off on a Boundary Waters wilderness canoe trip. You've been planning and looking forward to your trip for months, maybe years, and now the time has come. Ahead of you lies a remarkable realm of boreal forests, granite outcroppings and sky-blue lakes, a landscape that promises solitude, quiet and adventure. Although not undisturbed by humans, the Boundary Waters Canoe Area Wilderness is close to its natural state, in many ways unchanged since the most recent glacier retreated ten thousand years ago. It's a magical place, an environment of wonder, beauty, mystery and sometimes danger. And even when you find solitude as you penetrate this 1.1-million-acre wilderness, you feel the world around you. As Sigurd Olson says in a 1980 documentary film, *The Wilderness World of Sigurd F. Olson*, "This little corner of wilderness epitomizes all the wilderness any place in the world."

If this is your first trip to the Boundary Waters Canoe Area Wilderness, what do you think you will most enjoy? If this is a return trip, what are your favorite things to do?

Is it sitting alone by the shore and looking out across the lake or talking with your companions by the campfire, telling stories, singing and savoring those twilight hours in late August when the last light of day shifts north and lingers long after the sun has set?

Is it hauling your gear across a portage and doubling back on your return trip, freed from your equipment, feeling as though you're walking on air? Is it pitching your tent, chopping wood and watching the first yellow flames climb the dry shavings of your fire or picking blueberries in the late afternoon and tasting them on your pancakes the next morning? Is it doing the dishes, hanging your food pack out of reach of bears, climbing into your sleeping bag and then waking in the clear, crisp air of morning and being greeted by a companion who says, "Coffee's ready"?

Is it exploring lakes you've never seen before or returning to your favorite campsites and remembering the good times you've had there? Is it admiring a magnificent white pine and wondering how old it is and how many storms and forest fires it has survived or standing beneath a scraggly jack pine that your son climbed when he was a little boy? Is it seeing a moose, watching the chipmunks scamper around your fire grate or feeding a whiskey jack from your hand? Is it killing three mosquitoes in a single swat or hearing a pack of wolves howl at the moon?

Is it watching the splash your lure makes and following the rings that radiate in slow concentric circles all the way to the shore? Is it jumping off a rock cliff into deep, cold water, listening to the soothing rush of a waterfall or feeling the tug of a fish on your line as you reel it in? Is it relaxing on your campsite with a good book, sitting by the shore looking out at the lake, remembering the first camping trip you took as a child, swimming in clear, cold water, sunning on warm flat rocks, hiking, taking day trips without your camping gear or falling asleep with rain pattering on your tent while you're warm and dry in your sleeping bag?

Steve (the author) doing one of his favorite things.

Is it paddling out from your campsite to gaze at the night sky, feeling the silent glide of your canoe, reaching your paddle down into the water and stirring the stars and then falling asleep to the serenade of the loons, those extraordinary birds calling back and forth, their plaintive wails rising and falling across the water, across time, stirring some distant memory and awakening some unspoken desire deep within you?

Those are my favorite things. What are yours?

1

Debbie Ventures North, A Black Bear Attacks and One Ugly Fish

When a friend told us about canoeing the wilderness lakes along the Minnesota-Canada border, Debbie and I were intrigued. We loved the outdoors, and I hadn't taken a canoe trip since 1971, when my dad and I had paddled the Red River Gorge in Daniel Boone National Park near Stanton, Kentucky, with a group of engineers from his General Electric lab in Evandale, Ohio. As Boy Scouts, my older brother and I had canoed Missinaibi and Bascotasi lakes in the wilds of Ontario. Exploring, canoeing and camping were in my blood, but for the past few years I'd been busy falling in love, getting married, completing my graduate work at the University of Iowa and starting a job in university administration. So we contacted an outfitter on the north side of Canada's Quetico Provincial Park near Atikokan, and on a warm summer day in 1977, we loaded our gear into our green Opel Kadett and headed north from Iowa City.

I have since learned that the Ojibwe word *Atikokan* means "caribou bones" in English. Maybe it was better Debbie and I didn't know this at the time. The name suggests how harsh this terrain and climate can be, how quickly things can turn on you, even during the lazy, warm months of summer, when a calm summer morning can erupt into a ferocious afternoon windstorm that levels twenty-five million trees in half an hour, as happened in the great Fourth of July blowdown of 1999. In *Magic on the Rocks: Canoe Country Pictographs*, Michael Furtman offers the following description of this harsh but beautiful landscape:

> *The vast Canadian Shield, the huge outcrop of Precambrian rock that finds its most southerly exposure in northern Minnesota's Boundary Waters, and which sweeps north and east across most of eastern Canada, is a beautiful and often inhospitable land. Dense forest of spruce, fir, and pine cover much of it. Hundreds of thousands of lakes, sometimes linked by brawling, tumultuous rivers, and just as often separated by bogs or precipitous granite knobs, punctuate the woods.*

Although we suffered no major mishaps, our trip was challenging. Debbie was not amused when after a long, tiring paddle across a windy lake we had difficulty finding the first portage. We paddled back and forth around a peninsula in search of the portage trail that would take us to the next lake. The voyageurs, the French fur traders who paddled these waters from 1690 to 1865, gave us the word *portage*, which comes from the French verb *portager*. It means "to carry" in English, and we soon had our first experience doing it. Starting up the wrong path, we realized our error, turned around and reloaded our canoe before we finally located the portage and once again began to *portager* our not-so-lightweight portables. By the time we arrived at our island campsite, it was late in the day, and during dinner it started raining, hard. Tired, cold and wet, we climbed into our tent for Debbie's first night in the wilderness, leaving our dirty dishes and a pot of peas to deal with in the morning, with me naively assuring her we were safe from bears because we were camped on an island.

Unlike grizzly bears, black bears rarely attack humans unless provoked and usually not even then. There have been only a handful of recorded black bear attacks in Minnesota history, and two of those were by the same bear. As reported in the *Minneapolis Star Tribune*, nineteen-year-old Tyson Crowder from Maryville, Tennessee, was attacked at Wabang Lake, south of Lac La Croix, on September 14, 1987. He was one of nine campers participating in a wilderness survival skills course offered by the Voyageur Outward Bound School in Ely. He sustained a fractured bone in his shoulder and multiple lacerations, including a large cut on his head.

Crowder was stretched out in the sun by the shore when he saw the bear approaching. It charged without making a sound. Rising to its hind feet, it reached for his head with open claws. Before Crowder had time to think, he found himself in the wrestling match of his life. Screaming, "Help! Help!" he fought desperately to keep the bear's snapping jaws from his head, shoulders and neck.

"I started to swim," Crowder later told a reporter from his hospital bed, "but I decided I better not. Bears can swim, too."

When the bear dropped him to his knees, Crowder grabbed its nose and tried to twist it. He finally escaped when a fellow camper drove it off by pounding it with a canoe paddle.

The next day, the same bear attacked fifty-two-year-old Jeremy Cleaveland, a real estate agent from Minnetonka, at Lady Boot Bay, an arm of Lac La Croix, only a mile from the first attack. Cleaveland and his twenty-nine-year-old son James were preparing to load their packs into the canoe when James noticed the bear coming out of the woods only fifteen or twenty feet away. As with Crowder, father and son never heard a sound as the bear approached.

"I couldn't believe how quietly it moved," Cleaveland told a reporter.

Father and son did what you're supposed to do when encountering a black bear: they tried to scare it off by yelling and waving their arms. But the bear kept coming. Cleaveland threw a canteen, spraying it with water. Unfazed, the bear charged. The father ran for the lake, dove in and tried to swim but couldn't because of his heavy boots.

"I turned to see where the bear was," Cleaveland said, "and he was right on top of me."

Standing in shallow water, he tried to fight it off, but the bear grabbed him by the nape of his neck, forced him to his hands and knees and shoved his face under water.

"I thought he would drown me," he said. "I thought it was all over."

James dashed into the water and dragged both father and bear to shore, where he snatched a canoe paddle and hit the bear on the back of its neck and head. Finally, both men managed to pry the bear's jaws open. The bear ran, but only a short distance before it turned and began pacing back and forth.

Cleaveland and James dashed for their canoe and jumped in. Even then, the bear charged into the water after them. Fortunately, they were able to paddle out of reach in time. Although the father suffered bites and claw marks on his thigh, forearm, shoulder, head and neck, as well as a badly twisted knee, amazingly James emerged from the ordeal without a scratch. Both were fit from regular jogging, and Cleaveland credits their conditioning, as well as his son's bravery, for saving his life.

The next day, Department of Natural Resources (DNR) game wardens shot the bear, an eight-year-old female, as it was ransacking a campsite not far from the scene of the attacks. When examined, it was found to be significantly underweight—117 pounds when it should have weighed 150 to 200 pounds.

"It didn't have rabies," said Garshelis. "It didn't have a heavy load of parasites. There were no apparent brain tumors, no old wounds or injuries or broken bones or teeth. There just doesn't appear to be anything wrong with it, other than being underweight."

At first, it was thought the bear may have had difficulty digesting food because of the one and a half quarts of plastic debris found in its stomach, including thirty-five candy wrappers and two small grocery bags, but later it was determined it had swallowed the garbage after the attacks. What caused it to behave in a manner so uncharacteristic of its species was never conclusively determined.

Fortunately, no bears disturbed us on that rainy night in 1977, although neither Debbie nor I slept well. I myself feel at ease in the wilderness at night, but I realize not everyone welcomes the intimacy of darkness as I do. At intervals, I was jolted from my sleep by staccato reports of "What was that!?" piercing my slumber like rifle shots.

"Nothing," I would mutter, "just a little critter in the woods." And then, just as I had drifted off to sleep again, there would be a sudden tightening, Debbie's hand clutching my wrist, another "What was that?!" and I would mutter, "Nothing, just two branches rubbing together."

"It wasn't nothing," Debbie said finally. "It was *something.* If it was *nothing*, it wouldn't be making noises. There's something out there."

Realizing my explanations were failing to produce the desired effect, I roused myself from my warm sleeping bag, unzipped the tent flap and stepped barefoot into a pot of peas, the cold mush squishing between my toes like soft mud. After that, I declined to further investigate the mysteries of the night.

Awakening the next day to the sun sparkling across the water, I coaxed Debbie into going fishing with me. She had never fished before, but wanting to be a good sport, she agreed to give it a try. As she worked on casting and retrieving her line, I managed to snag two large northern pike using a red and white Daredevil spoon. One was a monster, a veritable leviathan, nearly as long as the canoe was wide, the biggest fish I had ever caught in my life. Debbie was happy for me and, mistaking my luck for skill, even proud. But she also was appalled to see so large a creature, with flaring gills and massive hulk, occupying so significant a portion of our canoe bottom. After she snapped a picture, with me holding my prize toward the camera lens to magnify the immensity of my achievement, I released it, and we watched it slowly fin away.

Her next cast seemed tentative. Then she reeled in her line, attached the hook of her lure to an eyelet as I had shown her to do and tucked her pole neatly beneath the thwarts of the canoe. She hasn't touched a fishing pole since.

Today, if you ask her why she doesn't fish, she'll tell you, "The whole time I sat there with my line in the water I was praying that nothing would bite my hook. Why would I fish?"

A few years ago, I asked her what she remembered about our trip.

"I remember you caught the ugliest fish I'd ever seen in my life," she said. "It rained. It was miserable." Then, after a moment, she said, "It was beautiful. It was quiet."

What I remember are long, slow paddles across endless expanses of sky-blue water, an incessant wind that ruffled and churned the lake and shook our tent at night and an unforgettable week of my life with a beautiful young woman who did her best to share my enthusiasm for the outdoors. I remember feeling relieved that the trip was over, surprised by the sudden, unnatural stillness inside our outfitter's van but also happy we had undertaken this adventure together.

Our 1977 trip was the first and only time Debbie has canoed the border lakes region with me, and it will probably be the last, unless she has a change of heart, which is unlikely. For me, our trip was my introduction to a place that grabbed a part of my heart and never let go. Years later, I came across a passage in a 1929 article by wilderness explorer and preservationist Ernest Oberholtzer that captures the allure of wilderness canoeing for me:

> *The moment you launch your canoe in any of these lakes, you are conscious that you are living in the past. The very air you breathe seems not to belong to the modern world; it is too full of the fragrance of forest and lake. Wherever you get out on shore, you find rock, not limestone or sandstone, but the oldest Archaean granite, just as the glacier left it back in the ice age and still bearing the marks of the glacier's retreat. How clean it is, and how quickly it dries after a rain and what a place for building a fire! Nor do the trees seem less ancient. They grow directly out of the rocks, their roots clutching a ledge or embedded deep in the crevices. Even the Indians you meet greet you with a phrase they have learned so long ago that few of them know it is not their own. "Bow-jou, bow-jou" carries you back to the days of the first French songs.*

Exploring the Quetico wilderness was more than a nice vacation for me. It was also an opportunity to paddle back in time and glimpse a part of our continent's history.

The following year, 1978, my dad and older brother, Larry, took Debbie's place, and after that, Dad and I, along with various family members and friends, canoed together until 2003, when at the age of seventy-eight Dad said he had taken his last trip. To my surprise and delight, after a three-year hiatus he changed his mind and went on two more trips. Then, in 2007, after twenty-nine trips (including the 1971 trip down the Red River Gorge and a 1981 trip on the Namekagon River), he called it quits at the age of eighty-two. Now, as I look back, I realize how fortunate I was to have a wife who explored this "maze of bewildering beauty" with me and a father who took the time to canoe with me year after year. As I look forward, I'm counting on friends and younger family members to continue the tradition. If I continue canoeing the Boundary Waters Canoe Area Wilderness for as long as my dad did, I will have paddled these open waters and walked these pine-scented portage trails for half a century. I hope I make it that long.

2

In Search of a Whole, Live Moose

Our son, Eddy, got off to a late start. Not only was he born three weeks late, but once things finally got rolling it took him twenty-three hours to make his grand entrance. His mother and I agreed it was worth the wait, but being the restless type, I was impatient for him to become old enough to canoe with me, so I held off for as long as I could stand it and then took him on his first Boundary Waters wilderness trip in 1983, when he was four years old. Because he had been hearing about my canoe trips for as long as he could remember, the words "Boundary Waters" were an early addition to his vocabulary. He considered it a major achievement to be old enough to go along with his daddy and grandpa.

We had given careful thought to whether Eddy was old enough for a wilderness trip. The greatest dangers, we figured, were his getting lost, getting burned around the cooking fire, suffering hypothermia and drowning. The wildlife, Dad and I assured Debbie, posed no real threat. There were no poisonous snakes in the Boundary Waters wilderness, the wolves wouldn't come near a human and an encounter with a she-bear and her cubs was unlikely. The most dangerous animal in the North Woods was the bull moose, and it was a threat only during the fall rutting season, when it becomes ill-tempered and unpredictable. (In recent years, cougars, which are known to attack humans, have been sighted.)

The three of us took off in Dad's Cessna 172 from Flying Cloud airport and headed for Devil's Track Lake Airport near Grand Marais on the North Shore of Lake Superior. Once aloft, I looked down at a landscape

About to embark in Dad's Cessna.

dotted with lakes that looked like silver puddles in a broken road. Heading north, we followed the St. Croix River and then veered northeast over the forests of Wisconsin. In the distance, the Namekagon River threaded its way toward the blue expanse of the St. Croix flowage.

"On a relatively clear day like this," Dad said above the roar of the engine, "you can see about seventy-five miles."

Below us, the white dots of sailboats skimmed across the surface of Lake Superior. In the distance, the Apostle Islands huddled along the southern shore. If we crash-landed, I thought, our chances of surviving were slim. I couldn't stop thinking about how cold that forty-degree water would feel or how long it would take for a passing freighter or sailboat to come to our rescue—assuming we survived the crash landing. But I also knew my apprehension was nothing compared to what Dad must have felt in the Second World War. As a nineteen-year-old Army Air Corps pilot, he had flown a C-47 transport plane over "the Hump" of the Himalayan Mountains between Burma and China. To avoid detection by the Japanese occupiers, he would take off in the dark and fly by compass, with no ground radio navigational aids. At first light, he would search for landmarks to figure out his location, hoping not to have strayed behind enemy lines.

As we flew over Tofte, the terrain became hillier, almost mountainous. Rising from the water near the distant Canadian border was Isle Royale, the ragged edge of a sheet of bedrock that had been bent and thrust upward ten thousand years ago by the unimaginable weight of an encroaching and retreating glacier. Directly below us, the jutting rocks went from brown to turquoise before disappearing into cobalt-blue water. Along the shore were some new resorts, and on a hill a few miles inland was a cluster of buildings, perhaps condominiums. They were attractive enough, but I worried they might represent the first stage of a larger, irreversible development. As I looked inland over the dark hills of the Sawtooth Mountains, I hoped the unspoiled beauty of the Boundary Waters wilderness was safe from the banality of gas stations and shopping malls.

"That should be Devil's Track Lake," said Dad, pointing to a long, thin lake not far inland. If our plane had had pontoons, we could have landed on the water.

After a bumpy landing on the grass airstrip, I climbed out of the airplane. Relieved to be on the ground, I filled my lungs with air that smelled of sun-baked grass and dirt. As we unloaded our things, we were greeted by Bill Hansen of the Sawbill Canoe Outfitters. With him were two of his children, Ruthie and Adam. The boy, just a toddler, had a line of nasty-looking insect bites across his forehead.

As we headed down the Sawbill Trail, Bill said we were in luck. This was the first really warm day of the season. In response to our questions, he told us he was four when his parents Frank and Mary Alice had taken over the canoe outfitting business from the old Sawbill Resort. Soon, he and his wife, Cindy, would take over the operation, he said. He talked about his plans to remodel the buildings and expand the operation.

"I have some ideas," he said. "You've got to expand to keep up with the competition."

At the outfitters, we bought a package of freeze-dried peas and carrots to round out one of our dinners. We rented a canoe, paddles and life jackets. The canoe, a sixty-eight-pound Alumacraft equipped with a yoke and shoulder pads for portaging, cost us eight dollars a day. The rest of our equipment we had packed ourselves.

As we hauled our gear down the gravel road to the lake, Eddy began to fill his treasure case. At home, he was always picking up junk from the sidewalks and parking lots—bottle caps and pebbles and pieces of rubber—so I had provided him with a red plastic fishing lure case for whatever things he might find in the Boundary Waters wilderness. Through the clear plastic lid I saw some moss, two little pinecones, a couple twigs and the tiny gray shell of a snail.

With Eddy sitting in the front bay leaning against the center thwart and the heavy equipment loaded behind him, we pushed off. The first strokes of the paddle required conscious effort. Then I fell into a familiar rhythm, and my arms seemed to move of their own accord. Florence Page Jaques describes the sensation in *Canoe Country*: with "the monotony of the dip, the push, and the swing," there comes "a peculiar fascination" so that "the paddle, the canoe, and I were all one."

In the first stretch of open water, we saw a mother loon with her brown, fuzzy baby riding on her back. Eddy did a loon call he had been practicing but got no response.

It was already afternoon by the time we hauled our gear across the short, wide portage from Sawbill to Alton. As we pushed off into Alton, I marveled at the water clarity. Alton is a spring-fed lake. As with Sawbill, the water is so clear you can see down fifteen or twenty feet to the pale stones and fallen trees resting on its bottom. We rounded a long peninsula with tall white pines and then turned south and followed the shoreline. When we saw an open site on the east shore near the old hiking trail that leads to the Sawbill Trail, we decided to call it home.

As Dad and I unloaded our gear and busied ourselves with camp chores, Eddy raced around the campsite gathering sticks for the fire, climbing rocks and shouting, "I'm a mountain gorilla! I'm a mountain gorilla!"

Dad gave me a look.

"Don't worry," I said. "He'll settle down."

For dinner, we had our customary first meal: steak, baked potatoes, green beans and butterscotch pudding. When everything else was ready, I lifted the steaks off the fire grate, careful not to let them slip through the wide spaces between bars. To complement the steak, Dad had brought some red wine in a plastic jug. When empty, the jug would serve as a water container. We happily shoved the charred and half-raw chunks of meat into our mouths and slurped the runny pudding from our cups. As I savored our delicious dinner, I thought of canoe guide Bill Magie, who would replenish his energy after a trip by visiting his favorite restaurant and ordering "a canoe-tripper's delight":

> *First thing when I come in from a trip, I go to Vertin's Restaurant in Ely. I tell Matt, the young Vertin, "Gimme a canoe-tripper's delight right now." That's two T-bone steaks with a layer of peanut butter in between.*

Someday I'll have to try one.

Eddy settling down in his wilderness home.

With no breeze, at dusk the mosquitoes came out in force. We hurried through cleanup and slipped into the tent, quickly zipping the screened flap behind us. Then we changed from our wood smoke–scented clothes into our long underwear. In mid-June, it could easily get down to forty degrees during the night.

When I awoke the next morning, Dad was already up. Taking care not to wake Eddy, I climbed out of the tent and stretched, a little stiff from my night on the ground. The low, fast-moving clouds reminded me of how changeable Boundary Waters weather can be. On a number of occasions, Dad and I have paddled in the rain with the sun shining down on us.

Dad had already started the fire and put on the coffeepot and a pan of water for cleanup. A planner and an organizer by nature, he likes working and fussing around the campsite. As I was cooking dinner the night before, he had chopped and split wood, stacked it and carefully covered it with plastic to keep it dry. This morning, I noticed he had moved my wet tennis shoes from where I had left them to a spot on the rocks where they would catch the morning sun.

While Dad and I were frying bacon and eggs and toasting English muffins, Eddy made the rounds of the campsite and the surrounding area. He reported seeing some beautiful flowers and a few animals.

"Really?" his grandpa said, looking up from the skillet. "What kind of animals?"

"A baby moose and a baby deer," Eddy said.

"What were they doing?" Dad asked.

"They were playing, standing up and touching their front feet together."

"That's neat." I said, handing him his plate. "Time to eat."

Eddy sat down on the log close to me and forked half an egg into his mouth. Then he looked up at his grandfather, who was pouring water into the frying pan to soak it for cleanup. "Grandpa," he said, "I saw a python, too."

"A python? How big was it?" Dad asked.

"Big," Eddy said. "Huge. Sixteen feet."

It was mid-morning by the time we were on the water. With Eddy carrying his small backpack and two empty plastic water jugs, the first portage, 144 rods from Alton to Beth, went fine. (A rod is 16.5 feet, so 144 rods is 2,367 feet or about half a mile.) But the trek from Beth to Grace, 287 rods (or nearly a mile) and mostly uphill, was tough. When I heard Eddy crying behind me, I dropped my bags and ran back to him. He was standing in a swarm of mosquitoes, his fists pressed to his eyes. I charged, flailing my arms, angered that these creatures were attacking my son. In a single swat to the top of his white sailor's cap, I killed five. I hurriedly applied a fresh coat of insect repellent to his face, neck and arms.

"Come on!" I said. "Let's outrun them!"

On Grace Lake, Eddy's spirits were lifted when a northern pike struck a piece of moss and a pinecone he was dragging on a string. The fish held on just long enough to give the line a good tug.

"Can you believe that?" exclaimed his grandpa. "What a fisherman!"

That's when I noticed the baby toads in the water jugs. Thinking we would soon be drinking from those jugs, I told Eddy to take them out.

"But Daddy," he said, "they'll get away in the canoe."

Which, of course, they did.

From Grace to Phoebe there were four portages, none of them particularly long or arduous, but coming one after another they were tough. As I trudged along the last one, my shoulders ached from where the yoke pads (once soft, now hard as rock) were creating semipermanent indentations in my shoulders. It was then that I heard the enticing sound of rushing water. I dropped the canoe and stepped off the path with Dad and Eddy following. It was a small waterfall cascading into a pool of white, foaming water, like a rock-walled Jacuzzi. I stripped and climbed in. The water was shockingly cold and refreshing. What decadence, what luxury, I thought as I leaned back in the white froth of the current. Then I stood up.

"What's that?" Dad said, pointing to my backside.

My rear end was covered with dark specks. At first I thought they were little bits of moss.

"You have baby snakes on your butt," Eddy said.

They were baby leeches. Dozens of them. As I learned the hard way, leeches like to breed in white water because of its high oxygen content. I tried pulling them off one by one—Dad even helped with one or two—but at that rate we realized it would take all day to remove those tiny, slippery things. So we resorted to my old scoutmaster Mac's remedy: Dad dug into the food pack and pulled out a shaker of salt. Allowing me the honors, he poured some into my hand, and I rubbed it in. Like magic, the little buggers began shriveling up and falling off.

On Phoebe, we stopped on the most exposed and windiest point of an island to escape the mosquitoes and dug into our lunch of apples, trail mix and cheddar cheese and salami sandwiches.

We decided to spend the night on Phoebe and found a pretty site on the north shore of the big island just south of the peninsula in the west bay. After Eddy and Dad had gone to bed, I slipped the canoe into the water and paddled out onto the lake. The night was still, the water perfectly smooth, its unruffled surface reflecting the light of the stars. When I stroked the water, I felt like I was touching the sky. I'm not the first person in a canoe to feel as though I had penetrated some boundary and was floating in the heavens. In *Canoe Country*, Florence Page Jaques describes the same feeling:

> *It was dusk now, but a faint clear light still held. As we drifted back through the high reeds, great horizontal ripples came slowly toward us through the crystal water. It gave me the oddest sensation—our canoe seemed to be rising straight up into the twilight air.*

In *The Singing Wilderness*, Sigurd Olson describes the same ascent:

> *Should you be lucky enough to be moving across a calm surface with mirrored clouds, you may have the sensation of suspension between heaven and earth, of paddling not on the water but through the skies themselves.*

Their voices echoing in my head, I paused in my paddling, and my canoe gradually lost momentum. Then I took a stroke, and again the water and earth passed silently beneath me, moving of their own accord.

When we got up the next morning, we declared a rest day—which didn't mean we would rest, but rather than packing our gear and traveling to another site, we would spend the day fishing and swimming and paddling around in an unloaded canoe. Later, as we were drifting with the breeze out on the lake, we saw a man and a woman, who turned out to be rangers, in a canoe. They were on their way back from Poet Lake, where they had seen a moose. With the news of their sighting, we were transformed. We were now three boys in search of a moose. We spent a good part of our day exploring the long, narrow lake, climbing its bluffs and scanning the shore with our binoculars, but we had no luck. No moose.

Back on Phoebe, a bald eagle circled overhead. Soon, it was joined by its mate. Then we heard an odd chirping and discovered some baby black-backed woodpeckers in a cavity of a dead tree. Near the beaver lodge by our campsite, a beaver swam lazily past our canoe. Never before had I seen one so near. Its broad back was more than a foot across. We drifted closer, and it turned slowly onto its back and then, to our delight, scratched itself under the chin with its hind leg. As we watched this droll creature swimming along, seemingly without a care in the world, Eddy whispered, "Maybe he escaped from a circus or a zoo."

"No," I said. "This is his home. This is where he lives."

When we returned to camp, I noticed a string of red dots that looked like chicken pox on Eddy's forehead, just below the brim of his cap. Earlier in the day I had seen some insects that looked like large gnats buzzing around his head, but I had paid no attention to them. Now I realized what they were: black flies. Unlike mosquitoes, which prick, inject and suck, causing an itch that for most people lasts only a few minutes, black flies perform minor excavations. Though painless at the time of the operation, their bites result in welts that may itch for days. Seeing those red dots on Eddy's forehead made me question the timing of our trip. Although June was a great time of year to see wild roses, purple asters, columbines, marsh marigolds and other wild flowers along the portages and biffy trails, I now understood why so many people canoe in late August.

After dinner, Eddy and I went fishing while Dad stayed behind on our island campsite. When we returned (alas, with no fish), Dad told us he had heard something moving in the brush.

"I saw four legs and a dark, hairy chest," he said. "It was a moose, not more than twenty feet away."

Before he could get a good look, it had vanished. Thinking the moose might swim to the main shore, the three of us dashed to the canoe and paddled twice around the island but saw no sign of it.

That night, we fell asleep to the serenade of loons. Their plaintive wails were wild and eerie, a delight to hear as they drifted across the water and then reverberated from the hills and granite shorelines. As any visitor will attest, the Boundary Waters wilderness would not be the same without their haunting song.

The next day, we broke camp and continued our journey down the Lady Chain. On Knight Lake, we caught our first two fish, a smallmouth bass and a northern pike. I recorded the size of the pike at between three or four pounds in my journal, but now as I think about it, I'm sure it was closer to five or six. As I was removing the hook from the northern, a fish that is notoriously slimy, I lost my grip. Suddenly, it was flailing and flopping on the canoe bottom. Startled, Eddy shrieked and back-pedaled his way to the top of the packs.

When we reached Hazel, we were delighted to find all three campsites vacant. We chose the one on the south shore, the same one where Dad, my brother Larry, the son of one of Larry's friends and I had camped three years earlier. Camping there now made me realize how much my life had changed since Eddy's birth. Debbie and I had become parents to not only a son but also a daughter, I had changed jobs twice, and we had moved from Iowa City to Minneapolis. So much had happened between these two points in my life, and yet nothing here appeared to have changed.

I LOVE BEING in this natural setting. I love the sights, the smells and the sounds. In the wilderness you open yourself up rather than close yourself down. Rather than blocking things out, you welcome them in. You become more alert. In *Canoe Country*, Florence Page Jaques describes how her senses were awakened on a canoe trip:

> *How much more I notice the touch of things! The smooth paddle in my hand, the shock of cold water on my face, the texture of rough sticks and pinecones when I pick up firewood. The slimness of pine needles in my fingers, the springy turf or hard granite when I step. And the increased keenness in the sense of smell...the different way that early morning smells,*

and twilight. The changes one forest path can give you as you walk along, the scent of wet green leaves, and dried brown ones, of mushrooms, and crushed grass.

The most common Boundary Waters sounds are, in approximately this order, the raucous call of the blue jay, the hoarse croak of the raven, the urgent tremolo and lonely wail of the loon, the piercing call of the seagull and, depending on the habitat, the Old-Sam-Peabody-Peabody-Peabody of the white-throated sparrow. My favorite, the wail of the loon, begins suddenly, overtaking the silence by surprise and then expanding slowly, enveloping and defining its surroundings, whereas the piercing call of the jay interrupts the quiet of the wilderness in staccato-like fashion, accentuating the immensity of its surroundings. The two sounds pull me in contrary directions. The cry of the loon makes me aware of the present moment. The sharp call, call, call of the blue jay makes me feel restless, preoccupied, uneasy about what may be happening elsewhere. The blue jay's call had a similar effect on Sig Olson, who linked it to the uneasiness that accompanies a new season. In *Listening Point*, he writes, "It was a bright and sparkling morning in late August with just enough hint of frost in the air to make one question the permanence of summer. A blue jay screamed the hard clarion notes of coming fall, and in that sound was the promise of change."

That's it. It's the promise of change.

The next morning we were awakened by a thunderstorm. As Dad and I talked about taking a day trip to Polly, Eddy started crying. The thought of moving on was too much for him.

"Let's forget the day trip," I said. "Why go any farther?"

Dad agreed, and with that decision came a realization. We were free. We were not bound to push on or to travel anywhere we didn't want to go. By mid-morning the sky had cleared and the weather was magnificent, with temperatures in the seventies. We had the lake to ourselves, and for two days we loafed in its peace and beauty.

Eddy spent a good part of that time in a lookout tree he discovered near the edge of the water. It was a good climbing tree, a jack pine, with plenty of thick, low branches spaced just right for hand- and footholds. Once aloft, he had a commanding view of the lake. From time to time, he would climb down and report his sightings: a school of dolphins, a black bear and two cubs, a herd of moose on the far shore, two pirate ships.

Eddy beneath his lookout tree.

An evening paddle just before dark.

That evening, just before dark, I paddled out on the lake by myself. Except for a few pink billowy clouds, the sky was clear. I laid my paddle across the gunwales and let the canoe drift. As I looked up, I felt like I was moving at the same speed as the clouds, and I had the odd sensation of being tethered to them. I turned in my seat and saw the light from our campfire, a small yellow dot on a long, dark shoreline. Nowhere else was there a sign of civilization. There were no powerboats zipping by, no planes roaring overhead, no lights flashing atop radio towers. Dad, Eddy and I were completely alone in the wilderness.

Above me, the stars were flickering to life. In *Fawn Island*, Douglas Wood describes a world of both physical and mental reflections:

> *The canoe is perfectly designed for two seemingly contrary functions—floating upon the surface of things and getting beneath the surface of things. There is no craft more at home in the world of reflections—rocks, trees, birds, clouds, stars—or better suited for exploring the hidden shorelines of reflections within reflections. What does it* mean *that there are stars, more than the mind can comprehend? That there is a universe at all? What is the significance of a tree, a rock, a thing—*any *thing?*

Like the canoe in Wood's passage, my thoughts seemed to travel both on the surface and beneath it. Drifting among the stars, I questioned my own significance. Who am I? Why am I here? Where do I fit into the grand scheme of things?

Then, *ka-thunk*! I jumped, lost my balance and nearly capsized. My heart racing, I realized a beaver had slapped the water just behind my canoe. I took a deep breath to steady myself. Then something white flashed in the corner of my eye. In the shadows along the western shore, four distinct splashes moved from left to right. Turning my canoe to investigate, I paddled hard, but not so hard that my paddle would swish and break the silence. Although it took only moments to arrive, by the time I reached the dark shoreline, all was quiet. I guessed it was a moose wading in the shallow water. If so, both Dad and I had now glimpsed the lower quarters of two moose. Neither one of us, however, had seen a single whole one.

Back at camp, I told Dad and Eddy about my sighting. We were encouraged, but we had to admit our search wasn't going so well. We hadn't expected to see moose everywhere, as people once had, but we wanted to see at least one. When Ernest Oberholtzer and his guide Billy Magee paddled the Big Turtle River near Mine Center, Ontario, in 1910, they saw twenty-

Exploring the rapids leading out of Hazel Lake.

five moose in two and a half hours. In *Keeper of the Wild*, biographer and poet Joe Paddock quotes from Ober's journal:

> *On the river just below the creek they were coming out in troops at seven o'clock. From every direction they came peering through the bushes. Different colors—some nearly black, some brown and black, some brown with buff under parts. Light spot near the vent. Sometimes they walk with heads under water. Total count for the day of 6½ hours paddling—44 moose.*

Maybe our luck would improve.

We spent our second day on Hazel exploring the rapids and waterfalls by the west portage. Eddy was wearing his blue loon T-shirt and white sailor's cap. After exploring the deep crevices cut into the rock by the stream, we paddled to the southeast-facing campsite on the north shore and went for a swim. Lying across the smooth rock shore was a large jack pine. Judging from the brown needles still clinging to its branches, I guessed it had fallen recently, probably dropped by a windstorm.

"Watch this," Dad said to Eddy. He picked up a round, flat stone and, with a snap of his wrist, hurled it across the water. It skipped four times before dropping beneath the surface. I was reminded of the time nearly thirty years earlier when Dad had taken my two brothers and me to Winton Woods and shown us how to skip rocks. He was good. He really could make them fly.

As I watched Dad pick up another stone and hand it to Eddy, my past, present and future seemed to converge. My father was fifty-eight years old. I was thirty-three. My son was four. I had no idea how much longer Dad would live—another twenty years, another thirty, maybe more. But some day, he would be gone, and after I had lost him, these woods and lakes would hold his presence for me. We've had some of our best, most intimate experiences here. Although we've spent most of our adult lives apart, we've had these times together, and we've done so in some of the most beautiful settings I could imagine. I hoped I would have similar experiences with both of my children. If I ever came back to Hazel Lake without Eddy, I told myself, I would stand beneath his lookout tree—maybe in the fading evening light or maybe first thing in the morning with the sun sparkling across the lake—and if I were lucky, I would see those pirate ships that sailed the open waters of his boyhood imagination.

The next day we reluctantly packed our gear and began our return trip to Sawbill. As we paddled the river to Knight, the yellow petals of water lilies glowed brilliantly in the late morning sun, and a great cluster of monarch butterflies clung to the lower branches of a tree. We saw a beaver, a deer and—at the end of the portage to Grace Lake—a badly decayed moose. It lay half-submerged in the water by the shore. The carcass was covered with a mat of big black flies. The hide, where visible, was gray, smooth and hairless. It was a whole moose, but it was hardly what we were looking for. We wanted to see a whole, live one.

We camped on the north arm of Grace, a good distance from the moose carcass, but the lake seemed unappealing, and we were uncomfortable drinking the water. The next day, we traveled to Alton, where there were signs of heavy recreational use—canoes on the lake, voices drifting across the water and campsites worn by frequent use, the underbrush yielding to dirt, the birches scarred where they had been stripped of their bark and the pines denuded of their lower branches.

After dinner, Dad offered to do cleanup, and Eddy and I went for a swim. In the water by the next campsite, four teenage boys were horsing around. Still resonating from the peaceful solitude of the past few days, I found their commotion jarring. Eddy, I noticed, was watching them intently.

"Look, Daddy," he said. "*They*'re having fun."

Well, they *were* having fun. In fact, they were having a ball. Like most thirty-three-year-olds, I still thought of myself as a relatively young man, just this side of being a lively and rambunctious eighteen-year-old. But Eddy's observation made me realize I no longer played anything like an eighteen-year-old. It was a sobering realization.

At dusk, I left Eddy in the tent and Dad by the fire and paddled out on the lake by myself. It was a windless evening, and the smooth water reflected the starry sky. I paused in my paddling, felt the glide of the canoe and listened to the silence around me, thinking about the events of our trip—our lunch on the breezy point of the island on Phoebe, our day trip to Poet, Eddy's lookout tree and rock-skipping on Hazel, my nighttime paddles, those teenagers playing in the water. When I returned to camp and rejoined Dad and Eddy by the fire, a sliver of light caught my eye. It was the moon, partly obscured by a cloud. As the cloud passed, the sliver grew into a complete circle that bathed us in its pale light. Sig Olson described a similar moonlit night on the Isabella River in *The Singing Wilderness*:

> *The moon was full that night and the tent was in the light of it. Because the river ran north and south at that point, the moon shone down the length of a long, silver pool, turning the rapids at its base into a million dancing pinpoints. A whippoorwill was calling and the valley of the Isabella was full of its haunting music, a music that seemed to blend into the gurgle of the rapids, the splash of rising trout, and the sleepy calling of a white-throated sparrow disturbed by the crackling flames.*

Sig was right. To appreciate wilderness, you have to hear it as well as see it. More than that, you have to smell it and taste it and take it into your soul. You have to let it become part of who you are.

Our last morning of the trip was tough. We got an early start breaking camp but then had to wait out a thunderstorm huddled beneath a thick cedar tree by the shore. When I was handing Eddy to Dad in the canoe, Dad lost his balance and dunked Eddy's foot in the cold water. Eddy didn't much care for that. Then, on the short portage from Alton to Sawbill, the mosquitoes emerged in force, apparently frenzied by the rain. There were so many buzzing around us that Dad choked on one. Once across the portage, we threw our equipment into the canoe and made for open water, our arms flailing as we tried to paddle. Finally, near where we had seen the loon with its baby on its back, we left the mosquitoes behind. It was only a ten-minute

A tired boy at the end of his first wilderness canoe trip.

"I never knew the Boundary Waters were so…neat and nice!"

paddle from there to the landing, but when we arrived and began to unload, we noticed that Eddy, poor guy, was sound asleep. We emptied the canoe with him sitting there, propped against the yoke.

Then, as we were walking up the road to the outfitters, Eddy said, "I never knew the Boundary Waters were so neat!" A moment later he added, "So neat and nice!"

Well, that made my trip. That and what happened as we were heading down the Sawbill Trail toward Devil's Track Lake. Some eighty feet ahead of us, a large, dark form lumbered across the gravel road. Our driver slowed so that we could get a good look.

There, finally, we saw what we had been looking for: a whole, live moose.

3

Another Moose, Two Black Bears, One Dramatic Rescue and a Remembered Image of the Natural World

Eddy took his second trip with Dad and me in 1985, when he was six years old. We were picked up at the Skyport Lodge at Devil's Track Lake by Cindy Hansen of the Sawbill Canoe Outfitters. As we drove up the Sawbill Trail, we saw a hawk, two partridges, a moose, a doe and two fawns—all before we had even begun canoeing.

Cindy told us we had come at a good time. This was the lull before Labor Day weekend. She said people were seeing lots of wildlife, and she warned us that the bears were hungry this year because the blueberry crop had been a bust. That meant the bears would be especially interested in our food pack. When we saw Bill at the outfitters, he told us a bear was making the rounds of the campsites on north Sawbill and Smoke Lake. Around Beth, there was an even more troublesome sow that seemed desperate to feed her two cubs. With Bill's warning in mind, we decided to head north to Cherokee and then loop east back to Sawbill.

Our first night, we camped on the north end of Sawbill. As we were making camp—no surprise—a black bear walked right onto our campsite in broad daylight. It was moving quickly toward our food pack and toward Eddy, who was nearby. Eddy looked up and froze. Dad whooped, and I charged, clapping my hands and yelling in what I intended to be a ferocious manner. The bear turned reluctantly, looked us over and then ambled off into the woods. To intimidate it so that it wouldn't return, I chased it a few steps. If the occasion warranted, however, I was prepared to execute a quick about-face.

Staging in front of the Quonset hut.

A short time later, we heard voices. Two men were yelling on an island campsite across the water. Their intermittent shouts continued for more than an hour. We wondered why the bear was pestering them rather than us when they were the ones who had taken the precaution of camping on an island. Maybe it had gotten a taste of their food. As the men hollered and banged pots together, I wondered how Debbie and our four-year-old daughter, Kate, would react to a bear encounter. I suspected Debbie would respond as Florence Page Jaques did when her husband Lee showed her an exciting discovery—a bear had been overturning rocks in search of ants, just by their tent. "I was *not* amused," she wrote in *Canoe Country*. "What if it comes back for an ant it has overlooked?"

THE NEXT DAY we paddled and portaged to Ada. We stopped for a swim and lunch on a small rock island near the north shore. We had just finished our peanut butter and jelly sandwiches when Eddy got too close to the steep granite ledge and started sliding. Once he was in motion, there was no stopping. Down he went, six feet, splashing into the freezing cold water.

"Ooh! Ooh! Ooh!" he gasped, dog-paddling with one hand and holding his fishing pole above his head with the other.

I leaned out over the water and tried to grab him, but the shore was too steep for me to get near enough to reach him. Then I heard a splash. Dad had jumped in. He grabbed Eddy by the arm and tried to hand him up to me, but I couldn't reach him, so I snatched a canoe paddle by the blade and held out the handle. Eddy caught it and held tight with one hand, the other still clutching his fishing rod. With Dad boosting him from the rear, I pulled him up the rock ledge. Then Dad swam to where the shore was less steep and scrambled out. Both grandfather and grandson were wet and cold.

As Dad changed into dry clothes, I helped Eddy into his.

"Why didn't you just swim back to shore?" I asked. I was thankful and relieved he was all right but perplexed by his behavior.

"I didn't want to let go of my pole," he said. "I was going to hold my breath and swim with one hand when Grandpa jumped in."

After Dad and Eddy had warmed up, we traveled on to Skoop. On the other side of that tiny lake lay the arduous 180-rod portage to Cherokee. The challenge wasn't the distance, little more than half a mile, but the terrain. As Bill Hansen points out on his annotated map, that portage takes you over the Laurentian Divide. "These hills which are causing you to grunt and sweat under your pack," he writes, "are also dividing the watershed between the Atlantic and Arctic Oceans." It was over this ridge dividing two oceans that Eddy carried his life jacket, backpack, tackle box and cook kit—a significantly heavier load than he had carried two years earlier.

On the narrows leading to the south end of Cherokee, we looked up and saw a small bear perched on a bluff gazing down at us. We paused in our paddling and watched it as it watched us. Then it turned and vanished into the forest, and in that moment I realized that seeing a large animal in the wild is very different from seeing one in a zoo enclosure, behind a fence or glass barrier. The bear had appeared and disappeared, announcing its presence without a sound. The rock and surrounding trees where it had stood now seemed wilder and more remote, the wilderness deeper, the silence more complete.

We found a lovely site on a granite point overlooking Cherokee, the first one on the west shore after the portage from Skoop. As I fell asleep that night, I felt grateful that things had turned out well. It wasn't every day your father jumps into a lake to save your son's life.

We were so taken with the beauty of Cherokee—with its clear water, many islands, steep shorelines and granite outcroppings—that we decided to spend a second day and night there. It felt good to slow down and relax.

Although it had clouded over the day before, today was sunny and beautiful. We loafed by the campsite, sunbathed on the big flat rock and swam naked in the cold, rejuvenating water of the Boundary Waters wilderness.

After lunch, Dad took Eddy fishing. I stayed on the campsite, writing in my journal and watching them out on the lake while chipmunks hopped up and down from the picnic table. I had shaved after breakfast, and I felt clean and warm in the afternoon sun. Drowsy, I lay back on the warm rock and closed my eyes. The breeze rustled the aspen leaves overhead. Occasionally, a fly or a bee buzzed by. Those were the only sounds.

NOW THE WAIL of a loon is rising in the distance. A chipmunk startles me when it bounces across my knee and hurries on its way, heedless of my presence. A slate-colored junco hops across the campsite. I hope Dad and Eddy catch something.

We're seeing more loons than in previous years, singing at all times of the day rather than just at night. Common loons are such an extraordinary animal. In *Loon Magic*, Tom Klein laments that such a fascinating bird was given such an uninspiring name:

> *Of the four species of loons, the three of the far north—the arctic, yellow-billed, and red-throated loons—carry proud, descriptive names. But is the other loon really "common"? To most, it's a spectacular bird...Perhaps the number of "other" names for the common loon have been a response to this injustice. The common loon has flown under such interesting names as the great northern diver, the ring-necked loon, the black-billed loon, the ember goose, and the walloon. By any name, the common loon is a special bird.*

Dad and Eddy are paddling toward me. "Catch anything?" I ask as they approach the shore.

"Not even a nibble," Dad says.

We've seen only one canoe on the water today. It was late in the afternoon when some people arrived at the campsite north of ours. The sense of isolation and solitude has been wonderful. Few bugs, few people. The lull before Labor Day weekend. Nice timing.

AFTER DAD AND EDDY returned to camp, the three of us paddled out on the lake, where we watched a bald eagle riding a thermal. With motionless wings, it circled and rose higher and higher on the column of warm rising air. Such grace and beauty. Back at our campsite, the chipmunks and mice were pests, but at least the chipmunks were amusing. As Miron (Bud) Heinselman points out in *The Boundary Waters Wilderness Ecosystem*, there are two types of chipmunks in these northern forests: "The eastern chipmunk's repeated low barklike call and the least chipmunk's repeated 'chip-chip-chip' notes are familiar sounds." Whichever kind was at our campsite, we enjoyed watching them scamper about. Eddy named three of them: Stubby for its short tail and Fasty and Fatso for obvious reasons. Later, I took Eddy out to a rocky point, where he caught seven leeches. He kept one for bait and the others for pets. I told him his mother would be thrilled by his collection.

En route from Cherokee to Sitka the next day, we again crossed the Laurentian Divide and traveled on to North Temperance and then to South Temperance, where we camped. As the sun was setting, we watched a beaver swim by, a slow-moving dot followed by a dark V in the illuminated water. The night air turned chilly, and we threw more wood on the fire. With Eddy seated on the log between us, we sat without talking, enjoying the warmth of the fire, watching its flames and sparks and listening to its crackle.

After a while, I asked Dad about his upcoming retirement. He had had a long and distinguished career working on jet engines for General Electric.

"What are you most proud of?" I asked.

"The William Badger Award," he said without hesitation. "I got it for being an outstanding material engineer."

"When was that?"

"In 1977, the year before we took our first Boundary Waters trip."

As Dad talked about the things he wanted to do during retirement, I found myself wishing I had made the trip to Cincinnati to see him get his award. I should have been there, but I could do nothing about it now. Some things in life, I realized, you get only one chance to do right.

A little while later, we heard a terrific splashing, and we dashed to the shore to see what was causing the commotion. Two loons—males in a territorial dispute, we guessed—were fighting out on the lake. Ducking under water, they came up neck to neck, charged, broke apart and then poked their heads under water as though they were watching to fend off an attack from below. Finally, they broke off their battle. As they parted, I imagined the damage one of those sharp beaks could do. Loons are gorgeous birds, but they're also fierce. If they think their territory is being infringed on by mallards or other ducks, they'll use those sharp beaks to eliminate the intruders, piercing their soft bellies from below.

The next morning, while we ate our breakfast of pancakes, bacon and applesauce, the sky cleared. After breakfast, Eddy and I went fishing while Dad did cleanup. As Eddy and I sat facing each other in the canoe, I tried to imagine a grown man sitting across from me. It would happen one day. And when it did, I knew it would seem as though it had happened in an instant. I hoped as I approached old age there would be more days like this one, the sun warm on our backs, the canoe drifting with the breeze and me sitting across from my grownup son. I hoped it would turn out that way.

I'M SITTING BY the fire grate, basking in the sun. I'm using a sawed-off log, standing on end, for my writing table. I feel a prick on the back of my neck. One quick slap from me; one less mosquito to torment humankind.

Thinking about the trip. Thinking about my life, my father, my son, about family, friends. Eddy is quite the amateur naturalist these days. He loves his Golden Guide book on pond life, a nicely illustrated pocketbook published by St. Martin's Press. When he sees a meadow vole running across the portage trail or a string of eggs on a stick under water, he pulls out his guide to identify what he's looking at. He's convinced that the northern pike that chased my lure on Ada was actually a giant salamander. We think the leeches he caught are of the Erpobdellas variety. At one point, he had in his possession an assortment of worms, leeches, baby toads and snails. He occupies himself around the campsite much as he did two years ago—wandering around, talking to himself, picking things up and examining them. What a gift to be reintroduced to nature through his eager, unjaded eyes. "If you have the power of wonder," Sig Olson said in that 1980 documentary film, "you are forever young. The whole world is pristine and new and exciting."

I haven't done everything right as a father and a son, but taking this trip with my six-year-old son and my sixty-year-old father is one of them. These annual trips make me realize how quickly our time together—and my life—is going by. Although Dad is still in remarkably good shape, he's getting older. So am I. And Eddy is growing up. There isn't much baby left in him. In some ways, he acts grown up, but in others he's still a little boy. When he fell into Ada Lake, he didn't panic and he didn't cry. On the other hand, his orange Tang mustache overlaid by a red Kool-Aid one makes him look anything but mature. Today, he's dressed in a red triceratops T-shirt under a red flannel shirt, and the knees of his jeans are patched. I took a picture of him sitting in the sun by our tent next

Left: A little boy soon to be a young man.

Below: Grandpa and grandson taking it easy in the sun.

Opposite top: Not too big for his dad to turn his world upside down.

Opposite bottom: A quiet moment with things to talk about.

to his grandpa. Then Dad took one of me jostling him, holding him upside down, and another of him sitting with me by the shore, deep in conversation. These chance images, these simple pleasures, give meaning to my life.

Just heard a splash. Dad's in for a bath. Think I'll join him…

The next morning we broke camp and headed south across the lake. At the portage leading to Weird, Eddy dropped his black Swiss Army pocketknife into the water. I had given him one just like mine before our trip. I tried to scoop it up with the canoe paddle and almost had it, but it slipped off the rock ledge. As I watched it disappear into deeper water, I felt like an inadequate father who had failed his son, who was now sobbing. I stripped off my clothes, hoping no one would happen down the portage trail at that moment, and stepped tentatively into the cold water. Then, turning my better side up, I dove. The deeper I went, the colder it got. I thrust my hands into the muck, but I couldn't find it. After several attempts, I gave up. When I emerged from the water, shivering and empty-handed, Eddy bawled, "I want my mommy! I want my mommy!" It was the only time he had mentioned his mother during the trip. I felt sorry for him, but losing treasured possessions was part of life, I told myself, and today my son had learned an important lesson about loss and the relative unimportance of material things. Then I gave him my knife.

As we continued down the Temperance River leading to Weird Lake, we were delighted to find the waterway thick with wild rice plants, their ripe tips purple in the sun. From there, we paddled on to Jack and Kelly. On the long 227-rod portage from Kelly to Burnt, we came across two rangers, a man and a woman, working with a pick and shovel to improve the drainage of the trail.

"Looks like hard work," I said.

"It's good work," said the woman. She was about my age and was wearing wire-rim glasses. "It's good stuff," she said.

Although this was by far our longest day of traveling, we had done a good job of pacing ourselves, and despite a brisk headwind, we didn't feel overly tired—until we hit the long portage to Burnt, our fifth portage of the day. We were hoping to camp on Burnt for our last night out, but all the campsites were taken. When we realized we would have to keep moving, we suddenly felt exhausted. Our map indicated that the next lake, Smoke, the last lake before Sawbill, had only four campsites. We portaged our gear and paddled out onto the lake. As we rounded the rocky point by the first campsite, we literally crossed our fingers, eyeing the shoreline and hoping not to see anything other than trees, rocks, a fire grate and dirt. To our relief, the site was open. It was not only the prettiest site on the lake but also one of the prettiest we had ever seen. As the sun settled into its late-afternoon descent, the wind calmed. To celebrate our good fortune, we stripped off our clothes and dove into the cool water, then sat on a smooth granite point soaking in the sun's lingering warmth.

We had an early dinner and returned to the point to watch the sun dip below the trees, too tired to feel anything but happy. In *Boundary Waters: The Grace of the Wild*, Paul Gruchow writes, "We have, perhaps, forgotten the connection between beauty and pain—the words awful and awesome come from the same root—until we have all day long battled a fierce wind blowing out of the west and, at last, with aching muscles, have made camp in some sheltered cove, discovering then the bliss that descends with the silence after the last light." With the stars blinking on, we headed for the tent. It had been a long day. As I closed my eyes, I listened intently, but I heard no sound, and I felt something close to euphoria. For Sig, "the singing wilderness" was more than sound; it was also silence. It had to do with "the calling of loons, northern lights, and the great silences of a land lying northwest of Lake Superior." He wrote, "I have heard the singing in many places, but I seem to hear it best in the wilderness lake country of the Quetico-Superior, where travel is still by pack and canoe over the ancient trails of the Indians and voyageurs." What a privilege to be here in his company.

The next day, we hauled our gear across the portage from Smoke to the east shore of Sawbill. It wasn't a long paddle from there to the landing, but it was tough going into the wind, and Dad was worried about flying in turbulent weather. As we continued south, we passed canoe after canoe coming in for Labor Day weekend. Our timing, in terms of both the weather and the traffic, had been superb.

"Cindy was right," Dad said. "The week before the Labor Day rush, from Sunday to Saturday, is a good time to be here."

"I think it's the perfect time for a canoe trip," I said.

As we made our way into the wind, I recalled how Eddy had fallen asleep on the last leg of our trip two years ago, when we had exited the Boundary Waters wilderness from the same lake. This year was different. This year, he sat quietly, lost in thought, alone in his private world. I leaned into my stroke and watched the waves break against the bow. I was in no hurry to leave, but I paddled hard, and it felt good. Ahead on the left, coming closer with each stroke, was the Sawbill landing, which signaled the end of our trip. I eased up on my paddling and looked to my right, where I could see a small pine-topped island and nothing but natural surroundings, a small reminder of our planet's perfect beauty. "The recognition of beauty is a kind of love, a love for all Nature," Sig said in that 1980 documentary film. I tried to fix the image of that island in my memory so that I could return to it whenever I needed to.

4

A Lake Named Night and One Ferocious Mouse

It's a cool August evening. Must be in the forties. I lean forward, holding my numb fingers near the glowing embers. The heat feels good. I stand up, stretch, kick the fire. Yellow sparks shoot past my face. I take a deep breath and gaze into the darkness around me, listening for the familiar sounds of night, but other than the sputtering fire there is only silence. The fire-lit ring of branches and shadows encircles me. In *Boundary Waters*, a book that Greg Breining did with photographer Jerry Stebbins, Breining ponders why we build fires and sit around them for hours:

> *Perhaps because it animates the darkness—the only actor on an otherwise dark stage. But I think there is another, better reason, and it has to do less with the fire at our faces than the woods at our backs. In the dark woods the fire is our last retreat.*

The year is 1986. Eddy is seven years old now, more grown up than on last year's trip. Still, there's a lot of little boy left in him. A few weeks ago, he lost his top front tooth, the second to go, leaving him with a prodigious gap, a goofy smile and a bit of a lisp. When he gets excited about something, he sputters. This is his third trip to the Boundary Waters wilderness, his third time walking the portage trails and exploring the lakes and rivers and waterfalls, his third time swimming in the clear, cold water and warming himself on the rocks in the sun, spotting eagles and moose by day, watching the moon rise slowly over the lake and listening for loons at night. Once again, Dad, Eddy and I have returned to this special place. We're like three children out for a summer frolic, more like three brothers than three generations in a canoe.

I move closer to the fire. It looks warmer than it feels. Overhead, the wind is moving through the pines. Their branches sway in a gentle symphony. Behind me the moon is rising. As it was last year, it's full—a mixed blessing. The shorelines are hauntingly beautiful in the silver light and shadows, but its brightness obscures many of the stars that would otherwise be visible.

A thin, wispy light moves slowly between me and the stars. It looks like a plate-glass window with traces of steam on it. At first, I thought the pale glow was the northern lights, but now I think it's a film of clouds illuminated by the moonlight. It's hard to tell the difference. I'm chilled. In one of his stories, Bill Magie tells how Native Americans used to laugh at the dumb white trappers for building one large fire on cold nights rather than two small fires the way the Indians did so that they could sit between them and be warm on both sides. If it weren't against the rules, I would be tempted to give it a try.

Yesterday morning, Mom, Debbie and Kate rode in the car with us to the Flying Cloud airport. After we had loaded Dad's plane and snapped some pictures, I turned just in time to see Eddy put his arm around his sister and give her a quick hug. She smiled, her blue eyes open wide with surprise, and then reached for her grandmother's hand. The girls had been talking about all the fun things they would do while we were gone. I could tell Kate was excited at the prospects of having her grandmother and her mother all to herself.

Just caught a mouse—a mouse, that is, not a moose—in the beam of my flashlight. The rhythmic sound of Dad's snoring is coming from the tent. The fire has died to a red glow. I'm tired. Should go to bed. But it's so beautiful and peaceful out here by the fire. In *The Singing Wilderness*, Sig writes about how a fire casts a spell and campfires attach themselves to memories:

> *In years of roaming the wilds, my campfires seem like glowing beads in a long chain of experience. Some of the beads glow more than the others, and when I blow on them ever so softly, they burst into flame. When that happens, I recapture the scenes themselves, pick them out of the almost forgotten limbo of the past and make them live.*

I like his analogy. I think of our South Temperance campfire last year, the one when I sat with Dad and Eddy and we talked about Dad's retirement. If

Kate (middle), looking forward to having time with her grandmother Margaret.

I blew on that bead now, it would burst into flame. It's a light in my life that will never go completely out.

At the outfitters yesterday, while Bill Hansen loaded the canoe on the van for our ride to Kawishiwi Lake, he talked about coming upon moose and wolves while training for Grandma's Marathon, which follows the North Shore from Two Harbors to Duluth, and about how he was looking forward to taking Adam, now five, out canoeing the next day. On the ride to our put-in point, Cindy gave us the news: Bugs not bad. Bears scarce. There still were blueberries. People had been seeing moose. Fishing was good.

It felt good to paddle. My muscles longed for that easy, familiar rhythm. As Sig observes in *The Singing Wilderness*, "There is balance in the handling of a canoe, the feeling of its being a part of the bodily swing." I know the feeling he describes:

> *When the point is reached where the rhythm of each stroke is as poised as the movement of the canoe itself, weariness is forgotten and there is time to watch the sky and the shores without thought of distance or effort. At such a time the canoe glides along obedient to the slightest wish and paddling becomes as unconscious and automatic an effort as breathing.*

I wonder if Eddy experienced that sensation. If not, he will one day. Today, he used a special paddle Dad had customized for him by sawing off half its blade and then rounding its tip. Eddy loves having his own paddle. When he strokes, I can feel his power. Son power. What could be more natural?

We paddled through the narrows on Kawishiwi Lake and turned north, and as we were passing through some weeds on the river leading to Square, we came upon a young moose standing in the water. Eddy spotted it. It trotted up the shore, stopped and turned to look at us. What a beautiful animal but—no disrespect intended—what an ungainly creature. I understand why some people say anything as strange looking as a moose must have been designed by a committee.

I lean closer to the fire. In *Boundary Waters*, Breining describes flames that "danced and cast leaping shadows in a little circle of light that defined our territory in the nighttime woods." According to Breining, "The effect of firelight in the forest is a strange one: All around is the brightness and glow of tree trunks, then, suddenly, blackness, as though the light had cooled and fallen to earth." But as I look around, I see I'm no longer surrounded by sudden blackness. The moon has edged over the pines behind me. It's surrounded by hazy gauze.

I like this campsite. It has a little cover on the west side and a full view of the lake in front. It has some nice rocks going down to the water and some fairly good-sized red pines. One in particular is convenient for hanging the food pack. The campsite on the peninsula opposite is distant enough that it doesn't feel intrusive. The Forest Service has done a nice job of spacing the campsites so that even when there are several on a lake you don't feel crowded. The sense of being somewhere remote is an important part of what the Boundary Waters wilderness is all about.

As usual, we're seeing lots of wildlife, including a good many birds, yellow-rumped warblers, a number of small, grayish brown birds (also warblers I assume), chickadees, whiskey jacks, blue jays, ravens and, of course, eagles and loons. What a treat to come to a place where the wildlife is so abundant. I am reminded of Florence Page Jaques' lovely description of what she and Lee encountered:

> *We have a great stir of wild life around us, in an extremely small way. Chipmunks by the score gallop around, mad with curiosity. Chickadees swarm in the pines, right side up or upside down, it doesn't seem to matter; their dee-dee-dee's are constant. Starring the camp are dragonflies of every kind, bronze ones, gigantic emerald ones almost as big as the*

chickadees, small ones of gossamer blue, which are my special favorites. And when I went down the shore to get driftwood, I ran into a migration of yellow warblers, hundreds of them, flicking in and out of the foliage like yellow sparks.

After dinner, Eddy and I went for a paddle. The breeze had died, and the lake was smooth. We paddled toward the sunset, our canoe cutting through the water like a knife cutting icing on a cake. Dozens of bats flitted over the water, coming directly at us and then veering off at the last moment. On the north side of the lake we came upon two beavers. Rather than ducking under water as they usually do, they turned toward us and circled our canoe. Although I was anticipating the sound, the sharp *ka-thunks* of their tails slapping the water and the mighty eruptions that followed made me jump. We looped slowly around the cove and then relinquished their territory. It was theirs, not ours. Then a loon made two passes overhead, yodeling as it went by. We heard some splashing by the shore and sat motionless, listening, but saw nothing. As we approached our campsite, marked by a horizontal column of white smoke drifting just above the trees, I had that sweet sensation of floating both on the water and in the air. We glided without a sound. Although our movement was imperceptible, the trees grew taller.

"Look at the stars, Eddy," I said. "Can you find the Big Dipper?"

He pointed to it.

"Good. Can you find the North Star?"

He made a few guesses and then admitted he couldn't. I turned the canoe so that we had a good view, and I showed him how to follow the trajectory of the two "pointer stars," Dubhe and Merak, in the bowl of the Big Dipper to the handle of the inverted Little Dipper.

"That star," I said, "the brightest star, the one at the end of the handle, is Polaris. That's the North Star." After he located it, I said, "Now, are your eyes sharp enough to tell which star in the handle of the Big Dipper is actually a double star?"

They were.

The next morning, while Eddy was sitting on the biffy, a chipmunk walked right up to him, its cheeks packed with nuts. The little critter must have wanted to use the trail and didn't care if anyone was there or not. After breakfast, Eddy set about catching leeches, toads and frogs, as he usually does on these trips. He had two toads temporarily contained in a stick corral, and I watched as he tried to fashion a cage out of birch bark. He pointed to the larger of the two toads.

“This toad got handsome as he got older,” he said. “He was cute when he was younger, but now he’s handsome.”

I took a good look but declined to offer an opinion.

Later, as we were loading up for our day trip to the Kawishiwi River, a leech attached itself to his finger. Because of its slime, we couldn’t get a good grip to yank it off. Then Dad suggested using the needle-nosed pliers, a tactic that worked, although the leech didn’t seem to care for it. Eddy put it in a clear plastic bag with some water and then held it up so that I could watch it swim in its curious undulating way.

“As long as you don’t mind the slime,” he said, “leeches are actually quite beautiful creatures.” He gave the bag a turn so that I could admire his specimen from both sides. “But you have to think snakes are beautiful to think leeches are beautiful.”

We had just come off the portage from Malberg and were paddling through the lily pads in the river when we spotted a bull moose on the west shore. Its full antlers, massive bulk and muscular build, so different from a cow moose, were intimidating. As it moved off through the brush, I marveled at how it could go anywhere in the dense underbrush with those awkward antlers. It seemed like the least likely animal to be able to get around up here, but apparently it did just fine. So we’ve seen our moose. Two of them. Maybe we’ll see more.

Our plan for the day was to paddle to Fishdance Lake, where the Kawishiwi River widens and there are pictographs above the water on a granite cliff, and then to backtrack and take the portages to Alice, but a headwind made for slow going, and we didn’t want to have another late dinner with cleanup in the dark, so when we reached the island with two campsites on it, we stopped at the southern site, took a lunch break and then swam, fished, relaxed in the sun and decided to go no farther. It was a good decision—it had already been a taxing “rest day”—but the change in our plan meant that the pictographs and Alice Lake would have to wait for another year. Next time we came this way, we promised ourselves, we would stay on this island campsite with its rocks and boulders and its panoramic view of the river. One day we would camp on Alice Lake.

The fire has burned down to a few lingering embers. It wouldn’t surprise me if it were two or three o’clock in the morning, but I have no way of knowing. I don’t wear a watch in the Boundary Waters wilderness. I rely on natural time.

While paddling today, I wondered what it is about moving through the water by canoe that is so enjoyable and deeply satisfying. Maybe it’s the pace. Although it takes a while to reach your destination, it's such a lovely speed to move along. There's no point in wishing yourself across a lake in a canoe. If instead you just settle into the rhythmic stroke and gurgle of your paddle, before you know it, you're there. When you paddle for the fun of it, you leave behind the speed of modern civilization and acquiesce to that quiet zone that comes with paddling. And with that sensation comes a kind of liberation. "Freedom surrounds us," writes Florence Page Jaques in *Canoe Country.* "We are finding more than peace here. This is an authentic and profound release from modern intricacies." When you travel by natural time, the world glides by at a delightfully slow pace, and you can examine it at your leisure. Paddling approximates the speed of walking, another natural pace that offers rich rewards, but with canoeing comes water, a buffer from the land that prevents too exact a measurement, so that your progress is gradual and gentle, marked only from a distance.

Fishing has been good this year. So far, we've caught walleye, northerns and something that looked like a giant blue gill, as well as a freshwater mussel that clamped onto my lure. Unfortunately, Eddy has not yet brought a fish into the canoe, although he's had a couple on his line. By his reckoning, however, he's had hundreds of bites, all by unusually large fish. Last night, we were fishing the rock ridge in the shallow water by the little island. Eddy was pulling one up to the canoe, but when it caught sight of us, it dove and snapped his line. The sudden tension and release startled him.

"I didn't know they could pull so hard!" he said.

Maybe because the fish had moved so unexpectedly and powerfully, or maybe because he was bare-chested in the cool night air, he was trembling. I took off my shirt and slipped it over his life jacket. Sitting backward in the bow seat facing me, he looked like an unhappy football player, benched after blowing a big play.

It's late. It has been a full and wonderful day. Yet even with everything we did, I didn't get a chance to read to Eddy, or to myself, or to lie back on a rock and watch the sunset or take a midnight paddle around the lake. Even here, away from the moment-by-moment demands of the clock, the days aren't long enough.

The next day, we broke camp in a steady rain and headed for Hazel. En route, a great horned owl crossed from one side of the river to the other and perched in a pine, so we were able to get a good look. Its feather tufts stuck straight up and looked like long ears, or—apparently to some people—horns; thus, its name. Despite the rain, its body was puffed up into a fluffy mass, and we were impressed by its bulk.

Between Koma and Hazel were eight portages. We skipped the short one before Polly by lifting our canoe over it. By then, we were tired and out of sorts, and our equipment was water-logged and heavy. Then, on the last forty-nine-rod portage to Hazel, the rain suddenly stopped and the sun broke through the clouds. Some friendly people on a day trip picked up our last load and carried it across the portage for us. As we arrived at the end of the portage, Hazel looked like a slice of heaven, and we were delighted to find our hoped-for campsite vacant. We pulled in, spread our things in the sun to dry and sat down to lunch.

IT'S MORNING NOW, our second day on Hazel. As in past years, we have the lake to ourselves. Eddy and Dad are off on a fishing expedition. I'm sitting under a jack pine, Eddy's lookout tree. I love the company of family and friends on these trips, but I also enjoy these quiet times by myself, when I'm open to my surroundings but also lost in my thoughts. I like getting back to the essentials, both physical and spiritual, reflecting on the events of the trip and thinking about my life and the people who give it meaning. And I like writing, as I'm doing now.

After lunch yesterday, Dad and I gathered firewood, plenty for two days' camping. Then we paddled over to the northwest campsite, where Dad and Eddy skipped rocks while I stretched out in the sun out of the wind. Eddy climbed out on the trunk of the fallen jack pine, propped by its bare branches a few feet above the smooth rock shore. He said he wanted to come back later today to finish making nests in its branches.

According to Eddy, there are two ways to tell if the fishing is good in a lake. One way is if there are minnows, which means there's lots of food for the big fish to eat. The other way is if there are no minnows, which means there are so many big fish that they've eaten all the minnows and now they're hungry. Sounds good to me.

Just spotted Dad and Eddy coming around the point by the east portage now. I hope they caught something. When they went off this morning and I stayed behind to do the dishes, I told Eddy to bring one all the way into the canoe this time.

After breakfast, Eddy played barefoot on the rock. He had no dry shoes because his second pair got wet last night when he slipped into the lake, so he lingered where it was warm and made motor sounds as he pretended to drive space vehicles over the rock surface of the moon. In some ways, he hasn't changed much over the past few years. He was playing much

Climbing a fallen jack pine on a smooth rock shore.

as he would have then. He's even wearing the same red windbreaker he wore last year.

Hey, his pole is bending. He just caught a fish! Grandpa is crawling toward him with the net, saying, "Keep him in the water! Keep him in the water!"

"My first fish in the Boundary Waters!" Eddy yells. "And my first fish trolling! And it's a walleye!"

In another first, Eddy canoed solo. He did a good job maneuvering the canoe going out, but unfortunately he had a little trouble getting it back in. As Dad and I watched him struggling with his sawed-off paddle, we had a few worried moments. With only one canoe on this trip, it would have been a long swim or a long hike around the lake through rough terrain to retrieve him and the canoe. Finally, Eddy was able to turn it around and make it back to shore.

Later, we explored the waterfalls, the ones we had portaged around coming into Hazel. We hiked up and down the chutes, waded in the water and climbed the rock shelves. At one point, I reached my hand out to Eddy, but he refused to take it.

"I can do anything you can do, Daddy," he said.

No problems going out, a little trouble coming in.

The stream divides into several channels there, and we ate our lunch on some rocks in the middle of one of them, the white water thundering in our ears. On the way back to camp, Eddy caught a northern pike. It was his first northern. Another first on Hazel. After dinner, I offered to do cleanup and suggested to Dad that he take Eddy fishing. Unfortunately, we had left the canoe bridged on the rocks, with one end in the water and the other on the shore, and as Dad was getting in, he flipped it and in he went. Though unhurt, he was soaking wet. So instead of fishing, he spent the evening drying his trousers, shirt and jacket on a clothesline over the fire. He kept experimenting with different methods, propping open a pant leg with a stick here, arranging a shoe there so that it would catch the rising hot air. With each improvement, he would comment about what a clever engineer he was.

As I made popcorn and Eddy roasted marshmallows, we watched for the first light from the moon rising over the lake. Then I looked at my son and my father, the fire, the clothes strung out around the campsite, the tent, the trees and the water and the moon, and I thought no campsite could be more beautiful. I love how close it is to the water. It has two sides, each marked by trees that are so familiar to me they're like old friends. One has an inviting crook, where on past trips I've spent many happy hours reading, as did my

From left: Steve's brother Larry (thirty-three) and Steve (thirty-one) at ease on Hazel in 1980, with their customary pile of split wood.

brother Larry when he was here in 1980. The other tree, on the east end, is Eddy's lookout tree, where I'm sitting now. By the fire grate on the west end there are a number of good sitting rocks, a fine place to watch the sunset. Last night, Dad called us over to the east point to watch the moon rise, full and sullen, over the trees on the far side of the lake. Because it was cool and windy this morning, we ate our breakfast there to be out of the wind and in the sun. In *The Boundary Waters Wilderness Ecosystem*, Bud Heinselman, who apparently had given it considerable thought, offered the following attributes of "an ideal summer site." I made a condensed version of those qualities:

> *A south-facing sand beach near the site, but not immediately in front, because sand soon winds up in tents, food, packsacks, and fishing reels... Location in an open stand of red pine with little underbrush, well elevated above the lake on a point or island, facing south, east or west, or north if the weather is hot. Canoe landing on bare bedrock with a gentle rise to the fireplace area, with safe sites to store canoes overnight, and a deep spot in the water near shore for obtaining water for cooking, washing, and putting*

out campfires (not drinking). Fireplace and eating area on elevated bedrock knoll with a good view of the lake. Tent sites on well-drained sandy or loamy soils back a bit from the cooking areas, preferably in a stand of thrifty younger pines, and tent pads well covered with pine needles. Toilet screened by vegetation and at least 100 to 200 feet back from the lake on a well-drained sandy or loamy soil. Location on an open bedrock ridge high above the lake yet close to the campsite to serve as a "sitting rock" where one can take in sunsets, sunrises, the northern lights, approaching storms, and wildlife. A location for swimming, with a bedrock shelf for wading out, or a sheer drop-off for diving.

Though lacking many of the features to make it "ideal," this Hazel campsite is my favorite, and Hazel is my favorite Boundary Waters lake. Despite the wonderful rapids leading both into and out of it, Hazel is by no means the most beautiful. It has no stands of towering pines, no islands, multiple bays, steep shorelines or granite outcroppings. On the other hand, despite its being a relatively shallow lake, it's a surprisingly good walleye lake. I hope word doesn't get out.

THE NEXT DAY was a travel day. We had a quick breakfast of granola bars, coffee and hot chocolate so that we could get off to an early start. Just as we shoved off, it began to drizzle. Eddy and I made the rookie mistake of not putting on our rain gear the moment it started drizzling, and by the time we finally did, we were damp and chilled. As we moved through the lily pads and tall reeds, surrounded by steep hills on each side, we talked about the lakes in the Lady Chain. Traveling from west to east, as we were, their names are Polly, Hazel, Knight, Phoebe, Grace, Ella and Beth. They're called the Lady Chain because all but one, Knight, have women's names.

"I wonder why Knight is different," said Dad.

"I know," said Eddy. "Night was named after an Indian woman who was born during the night."

I had always wondered about that inconsistency, so I was happy to have an explanation.

A little later, Eddy laughed when a brown-headed duck flew away from us in alarm on the narrows of Knight, landed a short distance ahead of us, flew away in alarm and repeated the maneuver, apparently without realizing we were just following the waterway. On the series of portages leading from Phoebe to Grace, we met an English boy and his father. The father told me they had recently moved to Minneapolis, where he was teaching in the University of Minnesota's College of Biological Sciences, and he had attended the University of Essex, where I had worked as a Fulbright Fellow the year before. It seemed odd for our paths to cross here in the wilderness. When he told us he was disappointed with the fishing in Phoebe, his tone conveyed the kind of annoyance that comes from being promised something and then not getting it. Talking with them made me realize how visitors to the Boundary Waters wilderness bring with them such varying expectations.

For me, spending time in the wilderness is more than amusement or recreation or thrill-seeking, although it's these things, too. I enjoy fishing, but my primary purpose is not to see how many fish I can catch. When I come to the Boundary Waters wilderness, I feel as though I'm entering a region that embodies an important chapter in American history. When I paddle across a lake or walk along a portage trail, I am participating in our heritage—a tradition of exploration, appreciation of the natural world and preservation. Our history, of course, includes the other story—one of rapacious greed, ruthless exploitation and shameless destruction—but we do have a caring, more enlightened side to our character, a side that makes me proud to be an American. And central to this side of our American identity—at least in the mind of Henry David Thoreau and others like him—is the Native American tradition. In *Once Upon a Wilderness*, Calvin Rutstrum writes, "While the Indian culture will likely not be assimilated in our frenzied society, it might suggest the advantage of much needed repose. We can afford to slow down long enough to allow the more profound values of life to catch up with us." Bud Heinselman takes a similar view:

> *The Native American people in the Boundary Waters at the time of initial European influence were still living within the natural system. They were not felling the forests, not clearing the land for agriculture, not introducing new plants, not decimating the wildlife, not altering lake and stream levels, and not disrupting the forest ecosystem significantly with unnatural firing of the woods. They were gatherers, fishers, and hunters, dependent on the fruits of the land and waters, shifting their small extended family groups and simple pole and bark-covered dwellings to take advantage of the subsistence opportunities offered by each season. They knew what the land offered and how to procure the necessities of life, but their numbers and demands were small in the total scheme, and the ecosystem continued to function much as it had for millennia.*

The drizzle was coming down harder as we paddled toward our campsite, and Eddy was getting colder. Dad suggested using the ground cloth from the tent to shelter him from the wind and rain while he was riding in the canoe. He liked that, and he said he did feel warmer.

At Beth, we made camp in the rain for our last night out. On his map, Bill Hansen calls Beth, with its clear water and necklace of pink granite boulders, a "gem," and it is. He points out that until the mid-1950s it was the summer home of an Ojibwe family. We made camp on the north shore, near the jumping rock and the 144-rod portage leading to Alton. The other three sites were taken. We were getting closer to civilization. When we pulled in—wet, cold and bedraggled, six portages from Hazel, the last one a 284-rod marathon—we were relieved to find this site open. We set up the tent, thinking the rain would stop and the tent would dry, but the rain kept on and on.

Eddy was cold and tired, his jeans and jacket wet beneath his yellow rain suit. I helped him take off his wet clothes and put on his red knit sweater and shorts, and then put his rain jacket back on, all the while the drizzle coming harder. When he balked at putting his cold, wet rain pants back on, I unrolled a black plastic garbage bag and pulled it over his feet and up to his armpits. Though not stylish, his plastic garb blocked the wind and helped hold his body heat.

While I was attending to Eddy, Dad busied himself making a patchwork carpet with plastic bags and his poncho to cover the soaking wet tent floor so that we could open our sleeping bags and climb inside. That accomplished, we stripped off our wet clothes and did something we had never done before. Although we knew the odor of food could attract bears, we ate lunch inside the tent. Then we settled in to wait out the rain. Dad slept, I read *Arnie, the Darling Starling* to Eddy and then he and I talked for a while. Then Eddy fell asleep, and I read Sig Olson's *Of Time and Place.* Still, the rain kept falling. Finally, we realized it wasn't going to let up. Dad suggested we skip dinner and call it a night. Eddy agreed, saying he wasn't that hungry.

With the rain beating an even rhythm on the tent, I slipped on my rain gear, unzipped the tent door and stepped into the steady drizzle. The clouds were thick, and it was already getting dark. Although the air was chilly, the rain splashing into the lake and dripping from the trees seemed peaceful and oddly comforting as I lowered the food pack and split some wood. Using my bone-handled hunting knife, the one I had bought as a Boy Scout while canoeing in Canada, I made some long, thin shavings, hunching over my little pile to keep it as dry as I could, the way my scoutmaster Mac had

Doing what you have to do when you're wet and cold, even if it's not stylish.

taught me. It was a struggle to get the fire burning higher than an inch or two, but finally I coaxed it along until it began to produce some heat.

When I thought it safe from being doused, I left it to root around in the food pack. I came up with a plastic bag marked "Friday dinner." Freeze-dried beef stroganoff, peas and pudding. Yum. As Paul Gruchow observes in *Boundary Waters: The Grace of the Wild*, "One piece of freeze-dried rubber tastes pretty much like another." Even with the big pot deflecting some of the rain from the flames, the fire sputtered and hissed. Finally, the water was hot enough to stir in the dehydrated ingredients, the pudding had come as close as it was going to come to setting and I was ready to serve dinner, although once again it meant taking food into the tent. I knew a hungry bear would not be dissuaded by the rain. Well, we would just have to take our chances.

I unzipped the tent door and announced that dinner was served.

"I can't believe you went to all that trouble," Dad said.

"I guess I *am* hungry," Eddy said when he caught a whiff of the food.

It was superb. With the challenge of the wet wood, the surprised expressions on Dad's and Eddy's faces, the spicy aroma of the stroganoff filling the tent—the fragrance made me think again of the possibility of attracting a bear—it was a truly memorable Boundary Waters meal.

That night, after Dad and Eddy had fallen asleep, I lingered by the campfire, fanning the wet wood, heating water and cleaning up the dinner pots and dishes, finding little chores to prolong the evening. I had had another good trip with my father and my son. These annual trips were a way of marking the passage of time in our lives. While Eddy was getting stronger every year, with more power in his strokes and more weight in the packs he carried, Dad was beginning to show subtle signs of aging. For the first time this year, he wasn't always the first one up each morning, and one morning on Hazel he had let me cook breakfast before he got out of bed. On the portages, he usually let me carry the canoe, although he hauled more than his share of the weight in the packs. At one point, he asked me if I thought he was slowing down any, and I said no, that he still seemed to get tired when I did. With luck, I calculated, he should have at least ten more trips in him if he kept his health. He would be seventy-one then. I hoped the allure of the Boundary Waters wilderness didn't wear off for him.

Alone with my thoughts, I rehung the food pack, light now because it was nearly empty. Then, before turning in, I stood for a long time by the shore looking out at the lake. After a while, the moon broke through a thin layer of clouds. A few stars twinkled. Maybe tomorrow would be clear, I told myself.

Finally, I climbed into the tent, unzipping and zipping the door as quietly as I could. Snuggled into my sleeping bag, suddenly aware of how chilled I had been outside, I lay there listening to the wind moving through the pines overhead. Such a gentle, peaceful, restless sound. In recent years, I have come to appreciate the different sounds the wind makes as it moves through red and white pines. The wind in the pines. Countless writers have described it. One is Frederick Manfred, author of *Lord Grizzly* and other novels set in the "Siouxland" area of southwest Minnesota. As quoted by his daughter Freya in *Frederick Manfred: A Daughter Remembers*, Frederick could hear music in their branches:

> *It's only recently when I was up in the North Woods here some years ago, just before I wrote* Milk of Wolves, *that I found out that those great red pines and those great white pines have symphonies in them. And it's not unlike the whales making symphonies in the ocean, very similar to that sound. So since then, when I want to listen to my own things I keep waiting for my tone to show up. If you sit alone long enough you hear your own tone after a while, not only your heart beating or your breathing, but something else…*

Something else? What? Something deep within us that harmonizes with the natural world? I wonder.

A loon begins its plaintive wail. The sound expands inside my head. As the last note fades into the distance, I feel as though I've been transported to some unfamiliar place. I love that sound. I never get enough of it. The song begins anew, its rising notes intimate, nearby, and I feel centered, at peace.

Then, something else. Not a sound as much as a movement. My imagination?

No. Something is in front of the tent, next to my head. I drop my pen and journal. I rise to my knees and aim my flashlight beam through the screen. Expecting a ravenous bear about to rake the thin nylon to ribbons, I brace myself. But I see nothing.

Then I direct my light to the ground, and there, captured in its beam, is a mouse. My heart skips a beat as the furry little critter stands on its hind legs and nudges the screen with its pink nose, apparently wanting to come inside where it's warm and dry and the aroma of food is so inviting. Overhead, the night wind moves through the pines.

5

An Old Friend and His Nephew, A Scary Pack of Wolves, Two Crazy Loons and the View from Eddy's Lookout Tree

In 1987, Dad and his longtime golfing friend Bill flew from Cincinnati, spent a night with us in Minneapolis and then continued by plane to Grand Marais. Eddy and I drove. With us in the car this year were my friend Jim and his nephew Buck, a year older than Eddy, who was now eight. Jim and I went way back. We had gone to the same high school, he was my big brother in our college fraternity and I was best man in his wedding. We didn't see much of each other these days, so canoeing the Boundary Waters wilderness together was a great way for us to reconnect.

Apparently taking the equipment list I had sent them as a starter list, Jim and Buck arrived in Minneapolis loaded with gear. I reminded them we would have to carry everything we brought over many portages, and we persuaded them to leave behind their large pillows, bulky full-sized sleeping mattresses, mosquito coils, canteens and their own cook kits. Jim refused to part, however, with his aviation radio, which he wanted in case he needed to send an emergency message to a passing plane. I pointed out that he was likely to see only a few high-flying distant planes or an occasional ranger's pontoon plane, but to no avail. We were still debating what to take and what to leave behind when Bill walked into the dining room with his small red knapsack, which was about the size of a grocery bag. He plopped it down in the middle of the floor and said, "That's all I'm taking." It was a dramatic moment, and it moved us forward in our deliberations.

The first two days and nights of our trip were a repeat of last year's route. We put in on Kawishiwi Lake and camped on Square Lake, an easy paddle after we managed to find the elusive northwest passage out of Kawishiwi's bays and islands. Between Square and Kawasachong, the stream was choked with white lily pads. As so often happens in the Boundary Waters wilderness, the weather was changeable and moody. Even with dark, threatening clouds overhead, the lilies were illuminated in sunlight, their delicate beauty accentuated by the imposing sky and rough terrain.

At the campfire that night, Jim and I told stories to the boys. On the other side of the flickering flames, Dad and Bill, I noticed, were listening, too. One of Jim's stories was about a psychology experiment on two mice to see if love or hunger was the stronger instinct. I was happy to hear that love won out. My story was a version of one I used to read to Eddy and Kate when they were little, about two young crickets who keep asking their parents, "What was that?" in response to every strange sound they hear at bedtime. Just as I was nearing the end of my story, a tree creaked in the wind, and Buck blurted, "What was that?" to everyone's delight. After that story, Jim and I made up one about an old French voyageur named one-eyed Pierre who would look for people to drag off into the wilds.

"He preferred boys, young boys," Jim said—and here he paused, looking meaningfully at Buck and Eddy—"boys about your age."

We assured them that the story probably wasn't true. It was just one of those things you hear around a campfire, we said. We didn't want to frighten them too much. Then I added, "Some people think his ghost still haunts these woods."

Eddy laughed. Buck looked worried.

Unlike Buck, who is ill at ease in the wilderness, Eddy is bold and fearless, loves every part of a canoe trip and is willing to try anything. When Dad and Bill decided to skip a portage on the way from Polly to Koma, Eddy said, "If Grandpa shoots the rapids, I want to go, too!" When he saw me chopping wood, he said he wanted to see if he could do it. When his mother saw a picture of him after the trip, she said, "That's not an axe he's holding, is it?" I told her he lost only one toe.

In contrast to Eddy, Buck is timid. Before the trip, Jim called me and put Buck on the phone so that he could ask some questions: Would we get lost? Would we go over any waterfalls? Were there grizzly bears? I told him I had been going to the Boundary Waters wilderness for many years and had never gotten lost (at least not for very long), and we always brought maps with us indicating the lakes and portage routes, so all you had to do is know which lake you were on and then find the right trail leading to the next lake. I also explained that if we came upon a waterfall or dangerous rapids, we

White lily pad flowers in bright sun under dark clouds.

"That's not an axe he's holding, is it?"

would take a portage trail around it and that the map would indicate where to find the trail.

"But what if you weren't looking at your map and you just came up to one?" he asked.

"It's not like in the movies," I said. "Besides, you wouldn't start down a fast-moving stream without looking at your map. If it were a slow-moving stream and you heard the sound of rushing water, you would paddle over to the shore and check things out. As for grizzly bears, there aren't any in the Boundary Waters, only black bears, and as long as you don't get between a mother and its cub you probably won't have any problems."

There was a long silence. Then he thanked me. I could tell by his tone he was unconvinced by my reassurances, but to his credit he came on the trip.

We took a lunch break on the Kawishiwi River, but the island campsite we spotted last year was taken, so we took a campsite on the north shore. We liked the spot so well that we camped there for two nights. On the first night, we were sitting around the campfire telling more stories when we heard a sound in the distance.

"Listen!" I said. It was a raucous howling.

"What is it?" Buck asked.

"Wolves!" I said. "Those are wolves!"

"Are you teasing?" he said with panic in his voice.

"Don't worry," I said. "Wolves are afraid of us." I didn't mention the rare encounters I had heard about when wolves showed no fear of humans. The howls continued, rising and falling in a riot of individual voices. "Listen. You won't hear something like this many times in your life."

Eddy was enthralled, Buck uncertain. He wasn't sure this was something to be savored. Even in the flickering firelight, I could see his look of wide-eyed terror. The howling lasted only a few moments, but it was hauntingly beautiful and indescribably wild. Then, just as suddenly as the howling had begun, it stopped, and we were surrounded by reverberating silence.

The next morning we broke camp, loaded our canoes and headed toward Polly. As we paddled near an island campsite, the sun came out and made the site look too inviting to pass up, so we stopped for lunch and decided to camp there. It was a good decision. Stopping early in the day allowed us to dry our clothes and equipment, and it looked like more rain was on the way.

As we finished pitching our tents, we heard a commotion on the water. We ran to the shoreline to see what it was. Two loons were hydroplaning across

From left: Steve's high school and college friend Jim, Steve, Eddy and Jim's nephew Buck in 1987.

the lake, one behind the other. They were flapping their wings and skimming across the surface, stepping with their feet but not taking off. On and on they went, beating their wings and splashing across the water for nearly a mile. When they changed directions, they threw up spray like water skiers making a sharp turn.

Later, we watched a mother loon feeding her nearly grown chick just offshore. When she dove for food, the fuzzy brown baby swam along looking about apprehensively and occasionally sticking its head under water to catch a glimpse of her. When the mother surfaced a short distance away with a small fish wiggling in her pointed beak, she stayed put while the baby swam over to her, chirping all the way. The transaction was efficient and businesslike. The mother popped the fish into the baby's mouth, and then, without pausing for after-dinner conversation, she dove again.

As we were waiting to see the next course served, we heard an engine in the distance and then saw a pontoon plane, probably a Forest Service plane, above the trees on the far side of the lake. Jim hurried to his tent and pulled out his radio, but he had left it on and the batteries were dead.

One of the things I love about canoe trips is that they allow everyone to enjoy themselves in their own way. That afternoon, Eddy and Buck fed bits of granola bar to a chipmunk, Bill looked through my Boundary Waters plants field guide and Jim read a novel by Louis L'Amour, while Dad worked at slinging a rope over a tree branch in preparation for hanging the food pack. Dad's method is to tie a medium-sized rock to the end of the rope. Then, rather than throwing it over the branch, he grasps the rope about a foot from the rock and slings it. Today, it took him three tries to hit his target. Usually, he hits it on his first or second try.

"This sure beats writing a contract on a Thursday afternoon," Jim said. Then Bill handed Eddy some of his sunflower seeds.

"Buck!" Eddy yelled. "Sunflower seeds!" And off they went in pursuit of another chipmunk.

In addition to these ever-present critters, some resident camp sparrows were hanging around. So far, we hadn't seen any mice. It's surprising how their populations vary from one year to the next. I wonder if owl populations fluctuate in corresponding numbers.

After a swim, Dad looked into a mirror as he combed his hair. "All I can say is that it took me a full sixty-three years to get this ugly," he said.

"Well, it's a good thing your sons didn't turn out that bad," Bill said.

Then the two old guys leaned back in the sun, each reaching for his headphones and stereo cassette player. Last year, Dad had brought a radio and played the country western songs he loves to listen to, and I objected to the noise. Now, with their headphones, they get their music and I get my quiet. It seems like a good compromise.

We've had few problems with mosquitoes this year. Whenever one did buzz by, Jim would pull out his can of repellent and improve the environment for those who followed in our steps.

Later that night, I noticed that Jim wasn't eating any of the popcorn and that Buck had eaten only a few bites. Then I realized why. Earlier, Jim and Buck had objected to our storing the toilet paper in the same Ziploc plastic bag as the popcorn. The end of the roll, I noticed, had specks of green moss from the biffy. Now I understood their reluctance to partake. I, too, would have abstained from eating the popcorn if it hadn't smelled so good.

It rained again during the night. Of all our trips to the Boundary Waters wilderness, this one had been the rainiest. Jim and Buck, as well as Eddy, hated putting on wet, cold shoes in the morning. To make matters worse, the ponchos Jim and Buck had packed were the flimsy kind you buy for one-time use at a ballgame, and soon they began to shred. By the second or third day,

Drying out on a wet trip.

they were worthless. On nearly every campsite, we had wet clothes hanging on clotheslines both inside and outside our tents. Stuck into the ground next to the fire we also had Jim's shoe-drying tree, a dead branch with smaller branches supporting one or more pairs of wet shoes.

That night, I took Eddy for a canoe ride. It was a windless night, and the lake was as still as a mirror, the water a perfect reflection of the sky. We paddled slowly, drifting in that shimmering region between heaven and earth. Then I said something to Eddy that had often occurred to me.

"When I die," I said, "this is where I think my spirit will be."

It was an odd thing to say to a child. I didn't want to trouble him, but I wanted him to know my thoughts. Then it occurred to me that my vision was a solitary one. What about Debbie, who prefers a comfortable hotel bed to a sleeping bag? Would her spirit be here with me? Would we be soul mates even after death? Was our earthly union a temporary one? Now *I* was troubled.

Eddy wet his hand in the water and watched the droplets fall from his fingertips. He didn't say anything.

After a while, I said, "Don't worry. If I keep canoeing as long as Dad has, I should have another twenty-five trips in me."

"And if he goes longer," he said, "you'll have even more."

I dipped my paddle in the water and took a long, slow stroke, and then Eddy said, "And you could go longer than him, too."

I hoped I would.

Normally on a canoe trip there's enough activity and challenge to take your thoughts from your worries and the stress of life at home. But not on this trip. I was having a hard year. Dad and Mom had separated. At thirty-eight, I felt like I was getting old. There were conflicts at work. And my relationship with Debbie had become strained. That night in our tent, my worries roiled in my head as I tried to fall asleep. I felt Eddy stir in his sleeping bag beside me. I rested my hand on his shoulder and took a deep breath. Then I pictured him sitting in his lookout tree, and I felt myself relax. I saw myself reaching for a lower branch, the bark rough in my hand, and I was pulling myself up beside him, and when I turned to him he was no longer a little boy but a grown man.

"It will always be here," I heard him say. His voice was deep, confident, reassuring. Then I drifted off to sleep.

6

Spectacular Lightning Strikes, Fasting to Death on a Wilderness Quest and a Perfect Day

On our first night out, we could hear the thunder booming a half hour before the rain came. Then there was a sudden gust of wind, the sky darkened, the trees swayed, the temperature dropped and lightning started popping all around us.

Everyone ran for the tents—everyone, that is, except me. In the tradition of John Muir, who rather than take shelter during a storm would climb out on a high tree limb to view the storm's splendor and feel its power and energy, I walked to the shore and positioned myself where I could see the sky, taking care not to stand under the tallest tree. With the rain falling in curtains and the white light flashing in the near darkness around me, this show was too good to miss.

Amidst the booming thunder, I heard a voice. It was Buck calling.

"Steve," he said, "I want you to come inside."

I'm sure he was genuinely concerned for my well-being, but I also knew he thought of me as his guide, the person who would lead him safely out of the wilderness. I watched for a few more minutes and then went back to the tent and climbed inside. In *Northern Waters*, Jan Zita Grover describes a similar storm:

> *The storm rocked us all night long; I realized then that I hadn't known how magnified the sound of rain could be when stretched across the tympanum of a tent...Over the howl of wind, I waited for the slow, toothy parting of tree tissue, the rushing descent of a spindly jack as it gathered speed to*

> *crush our defenseless nylon dome. My body hair bristled with electricity. As we lay in the dark, I reflected that I had overlooked some Significant Details: I hadn't bothered, for example, to bring raingear or to check weather forecasts. We were now about to pay for my oversights. The only things I had apparently done right were to put up the rain fly and to register at the ranger's station. At least I had the satisfaction of knowing that the DNR could locate our lightning-charred, tree-crumpled bodies days from now, when the storm finally lifted.*

Although we had not overlooked "Significant Details," I was aware of the danger posed by storms. A few weeks before our trip, I had read in the *Minneapolis Star Tribune* about two brothers, one from Florida and one from Alabama, who were camping in the Boundary Waters wilderness with their sons, thirteen and eight, when their tent was struck by lightning. The father and son from Florida died; the father and son from Alabama survived with minor injuries.

"When a person is struck by lightning, he isn't hit by a bolt like what we see flashing in the sky," Donald Kundel, the St. Louis County medical examiner, was quoted as saying. "He's hit by an electrical field. The lightning strike is deadly depending on how the current travels through the body." No human being is believed to have ever survived a direct stroke by the main bolt. Of those hit by a side branch, about half die. According to Kundel, the current of the electrical field that killed the father and son passed through their hearts and brain stems.

As reported in the paper, the surviving father woke up early the next morning, confused and unable to move his arms. At first, he didn't realize their tent had been struck. "I thought I was just stiff from a hard portage we'd done the day before," he said. He struggled for nearly thirty minutes to unzip his sleeping bag and then crawled outside and waited for the others to wake up. After an hour, he checked on the people in the tent. His brother and nephew were cold, and they had bruises everywhere. Then he realized they weren't breathing, and his son began vomiting. Leaving the two bodies where they lay, he carried his son to a canoe. It took him an hour and a half of slow paddling to reach La Tourell's Resort on Moose Lake. There the manager called for an ambulance in Ely, twenty-three miles away. Later, rangers from the U.S. Forest Service used a seaplane to retrieve the two bodies. When they arrived at the campsite and entered the tent, they found that the teeth of metal zippers on the sleeping bags had been welded together.

When I asked Bill Hansen about deaths from lightning strikes in the Boundary Waters wilderness, he told me that Mike Debevec, a doctor who lives in Grand Marais and practices in Duluth, once did a study. He found that people who died were usually lying down and were killed by "trailers" from the big strikes that spread out along the ground.

"Most had a small entrance wound in their ear and a larger exit burn on their heel," Bill said. "I know of two people who were killed while leaning against a large tree, likely from a direct hit. I've never heard of anyone being killed in a canoe." Bill said the safest thing to do in a storm is to squat on your foam sleeping pad. "You might get the thrill of your life," he said, "but you won't die." Bill has talked to several near-miss survivors over the years and has some good stories. (Bill has good stories on nearly any topic.) "A couple of years ago," he said, "my daughter Ruthie and I had a strike so close that we were slightly deafened for about twenty-four hours." A few hours later, he said, there was blood in his urine.

The morning after the storm, we awoke to a cloudy day, but soon the sun was shining in a nearly clear sky. Grover describes awaking after the storm she experienced with anticipation for the new day:

> *At dawn, the storm swept east toward Lake Superior, and a delicate stillness filled its place. The sun ascended slowly in air so soft and moist that the apricot light diffusing water and sky left them horizonless, unbounded. In this pink-goldness, spires of spruce and stanchions of jack pine hovered above the faint floating islands. Loons, much bigger than I had imagined they would be, hung dark and doubled in the water-air. I felt as if the storm had birthed a miracle, and I wanted to get out onto the water to witness it up close.*

Like Grover, I was eager to find out what the day held for us.

Our 1988 group was the same as it had been the year before, plus my brother Larry. After the 227-rod portage to Kelly, we had a long paddle through a narrow channel thick with the purplish stems of wild rice and the white and yellow blossoms of water lilies. Dad, Eddy, Buck and I portaged the 54 rods to Jack Lake, while Bill, Larry and Jim pushed their canoe up the rapids. Even with Buck carrying nearly a full load this year and a fourth adult along, the last two portages of the day—84 rods and 275 rods, between Weird Lake and South Temperance—seemed long and challenging. When we reached the end of the portage trail, we sat down to rest. I noticed Eddy looking down at the underwater rock ledge where he had lost his Swiss Army knife.

The next day, as we were finishing our lunch of salami, cheese and squished bread, another shower rolled in, and we dashed for the tents.

After it let up, it looked as though the sky had cleared for good, although we could hear thunder rumbling in the distance. We fished for a while on South Temperance, where Bill caught a good-sized northern and I caught two bass. Then Dad, Larry and Bill left for a day trip to Brule while Buck continued fishing from shore, Jim and Eddy went out exploring in the canoe together and I found a comfortable spot with a view of the lake and settled down with my journal.

Our trip is off to a good start. Everything seems right—the weather, the ambiance of the group, the beauty of the Boundary Waters wilderness. We're taking the same route Dad, Eddy and I took in 1985 on Eddy's second trip, when he was six, but we're doing a counterclockwise loop rather than a clockwise one—from Sawbill to Smoke, South Temperance, Cherokee and back to Sawbill. One change from our trip last year is that we're planning to take two rest days rather than one. I like the idea of a more relaxed pace, especially after those six portages from Smoke to South Temperance.

I've started reading Walter Farley's *The Black Stallion* to Eddy and Buck. I read the entire black stallion series as a boy, and it's good to share one of the books with my son now. Before dinner, we finished a chapter, and the three of us sat silently. I assumed each of us was thinking about the story. Then Eddy said, "You know, you don't even have to breathe in. The air just goes in naturally." Later, when we paddled out to watch the light fade from the evening sky, he said, "The water is like space." He has such a creative mind. I never know where his thoughts are taking him. Last year, he and his friend Brian were collecting metal scraps to build an airplane. This year, he and his neighborhood friend Jonathan reconditioned his skateboard. In just one year, he went from unrealistic dreams to a successfully executed project. He's such an easy and agreeable companion on a trip like this. I don't get this much time with him when we're at home. I feel as though I'm rediscovering who he is on this trip. It's too bad I can't raise him by simply having him at my side, the way fathers used to raise their sons.

I love the way he sees the Boundary Waters wilderness from three feet away. I see hills and vistas and stars, and Eddy sees leeches swimming under water and the veins in a dragonfly's wings. When he's in the middle position in the canoe and isn't paddling, he often drags his fingers in the water, making designs and patterns, watching the swirls. There's no use speaking to him then. He doesn't hear you. Today, he used his flat, yellow plastic whistle for a ski and moved it back and forth across the moving

Buck hoisting a canoe with a little help from Eddy (and another nearly hidden person).

surface. Although he spends a good deal of his time lost in wonder and absorbed in his own thoughts, he enjoys Buck's company. When the two of them were horsing around by the water this morning, they managed to fall in "accidentally."

It's good to be here, surrounded by people I love. Dad has been my loyal companion on these trips since 1978. Together, we have shared the easy joys of warm summer afternoons, faced the dangers of swollen rivers and storm-swept lakes and worked ourselves to the point of exhaustion on long travel days. My brother Larry has been my guide as to what to expect next in life. We were companions in early childhood, but our age difference of two and a half years grew wider in junior high and high school, and as adults we've had limited time together. This trip has given us a way to reacquaint ourselves with each other. The simple pleasure of sharing the adventures of the day reminds me of playing together in the woods at the end of our dead-end street when we were little. The people outside our family are special to me as well. I've known Jim since high school. His inquisitive intellect, playfulness and drive to succeed have inspired me. Buck is an accommodating, eager boy. I've enjoyed seeing his growth in self-reliance and confidence from last year to this. And Dad's friend Bill is a delightful, easy-going, eager-to-please companion. First up every morning, he makes a fire and greets me with "Coffee's ready" even though he himself doesn't drink coffee.

When I think about my life while I'm on these trips, I feel both the joys and the sorrows more acutely than I do when I'm at home. I wonder why. Is it the beauty of the natural environment? The slower pace? The lack of distractions? The complete absorption in the activities of the day? Maybe one reason people come to the Boundary Waters wilderness is to take time to reflect, to take stock of themselves and figure out what they're doing with their lives.

In 1987, two campers came to the Boundary Waters wilderness to explore the limits of their endurance. They were a twenty-one-year-old gymnastics instructor from Circle Pines and her thirty-one-year-old companion, an active outdoorsman. They went on an extended fast as a spiritual quest. They entered the wilderness in June with the intention of staying the entire summer. In terms of planning, they seemed to know what they were doing. They were traveling in state-of-the-art solo canoes and had packed plenty of food and supplies. After entering the Boundary Waters wilderness on Moose Lake near Ely and making their way east to Lake Saganaga, they camped on Gold Island in Red Rock Bay. On August 9, they began their fast. Their plan was to go without food and water for fourteen days. The man, who was six feet tall and at the beginning of the trip weighed 185 pounds, lost 40 pounds. On the thirteenth day, the woman collapsed and died.

Ancel Keys, a retired University of Minnesota professor in biochemistry and physiology, the man who invented K rations and is an expert on starvation, was quoted in the paper as saying a well-conditioned human body "can go on a lot longer than 13 days" without food. "But water is another matter," he said. "It depends on temperature and the level of exertion, but 13 days with no water or food is highly likely to cause death." Without water, according to Keys, the body begins to destroy its own tissue, and eventually the body's circulation fails.

Of the nearly twenty-three thousand camping permits issued annually, about a dozen were for more than six weeks. Of those, according to Barbara Soderberg, who was with the U.S. Forest Service office in Duluth, one or two people died in the Boundary Waters wilderness each year. Common causes were drowning, hypothermia and lightning strikes. Fasting to death was unheard of.

THE NEXT DAY, the weather was blah. We arrived on Cherokee early and ate lunch on our new campsite, but the unbroken gray sky left us feeling as though we had time on our hands without a lot to do. Everything changed the next day. It was a warm, sunny summer day, and we were on a gorgeous lake in the wilds of northern Minnesota. We passed our time fishing, swimming and paddling around the lake. For lunch, we stopped on a small peaked island just south of Mouse Island. (We call it Mouse Island because the campsite on the north end where Dad and I camped in 1982 was overrun by hundreds of mice that scampered over our shoes, up the rope to our food pack and across the nylon tent above our heads as we tried to sleep.) From there, the deep blue water of the lake spread out in all directions. The water in Cherokee was so clear and inviting that we had to swim. We jumped from the cliff, swam back around to where we had beached the canoes, climbed the rocks with dry pine needles sticking to our wet feet and jumped some more.

That night, while exploring the narrow channel south of the island and just west of the portage from Sitka, Eddy sat with me in the middle of the canoe while Larry and Jim paddled. We glided soundlessly along, absorbed in our surroundings. No one spoke. Then we heard an odd sound, a rhythmic scritching. Larry and Jim stopped paddling. Something dark was moving away from us in the water, with two white lines trailing behind, and we realized the scritching sound was probably a beaver chewing on a branch. Then, *ka-thunk!* I jumped, and Eddy whispered, "He could be cutting down a tree, so we shouldn't get too close to shore."

The air was fresh and damp as it was the morning after the big storm on the first night of our trip, laden with aromas of the night and the promise of things to come. I took a deep breath. From far away came the sound of the waterfall by the portage. Its sound was both muffled and amplified by the stillness of the night. It had been a perfect morning, a perfect afternoon and now a perfect evening. A perfect day.

7

Loon Stories and the Stakeout

After a pleasant, if bumpy, ride down the twenty-four-mile Sawbill Trail, we arrived at the outfitters at two thirty in the afternoon. This year, 1989, we were a smaller group, minus Larry and Buck. The first thing Dad did when he saw Eddy was give him his old foreign coin collection. Dad and his friend Bill were both looking good, although Bill had hurt his back a few days ago and was in some discomfort. As always, it was good to see the crew at Sawbill Canoe Outfitters. Even the buildings looked good to us. We found Cindy at the desk, and she told us the fishing was great, the mosquitoes not a problem. Before we left the outfitters, we took a quick tour of Cindy and Bill's new log house, which was under construction behind the store.

Unfortunately, it began to drizzle as a Sawbill crew member named Mary drove us to Kawishiwi Lake, and the rain stayed with us off and on as we paddled to Square. We found a campsite on the south shore, had the lake to ourselves, made camp and enjoyed our traditional first night's dinner of steak, salad, hash browns and runny pudding. We did cleanup by flashlight and then, still damp from our paddle in, hit the sack. I read from *A Wrinkle in Time* to Eddy—and to Jim, who told me how much he had enjoyed hearing me read Walter Farley's *The Black Stallion* the previous year. Then I snuggled into my new Slumberjack mummy bag (a birthday gift from Debbie), found it warm and comfortable and closed my eyes for a good night's sleep.

In the morning, I baked some blueberry muffin mix in a pot to go with our bacon and eggs. When I noticed the top was still gooey, I flipped it upside down into a frying pan to finish it off. It turned out well, despite some black carbon around the edges. As we were eating, a mouse ran over Bill's foot. Without hesitating, he stomped on it and then kicked it aside. Within moments, a whisky jack swooped down and snatched up the carcass. Then, as we were packing, an eagle flew by—a beautiful sight.

Despite the water level being low, we managed the portages well. I carried the canoe and two small backpacks on the 179-rod portage from Kawasachong to Townline without stopping to use the canoe rests. Feeling good! I love hiking deep in the woods and experiencing "the intimacy that is yours on the ground," as Sig describes it.

As we loaded our canoes at the end of the portage to Polly, we saw another eagle and shortly after an osprey with a fish hanging from its talons. The island campsite on Polly where we had stayed two years ago was taken, as was the one on the west shore of the peninsula where I had stayed with my men's group the year before. Fortunately, the other campsite I like, the one on the northern tip of the peninsula, was open, and we were delighted to have it. We arrived in time for lunch, with the sun breaking through the clouds. The rest of the day lay before us. Unscheduled time. What luxury.

NOW AS I SIT on the flat rock of our campsite, two sounds come to me, both pleasing: the waves lapping against the shore—"the chuckle of the water," Sig called it—and Eddy's occasional laugh. Jim is reading Max Brand's *Rustlers of Beacon Creek* to him. They're sitting on the rock point twenty feet down the shore from me. The air has a chill to it, the breeze is fresh, the sun hot, the lake water freezing (I've already gone in twice).

Eddy looks sweet with his buzz haircut, blue sweat pants (with the torn knees), maroon Minnesota Gophers sweatshirt and white Colorado Buffaloes cap that a friend from Denver gave him. He was delighted with a king-sized leech he caught at the end of one of our portages, and he is fascinated by Jim's stories. I've noticed how Jim's conversation stimulates his mind. When Jim asked him if he thought he would ever want to be a politician, Eddy said no, because if you ever made a mistake people would hate you for the rest of your life. He said another reason was that elected officials received special treatment, and he thought everyone should be treated the same.

IN THE MORNING, it was cloudy and cool. After our breakfast of oatmeal and applesauce, Eddy was whipping his fishing pole around down by the shore when the top half flew off. "I don't know where it went," he said, fighting back tears. "It didn't leave any rings. If it went into the lake, it should have left rings." I suggested we offer a prize to whoever found the missing piece. Eddy thought that was a good idea. "I'll do cleanup for whoever finds it," he said.

It was Jim who won the prize. He found the lost piece behind a spruce tree a few feet from the campfire, so Eddy took Jim's place doing cleanup with Bill that night. We kidded Bill, poor guy, who may have gotten the raw end of the deal, but Bill worked with Eddy patiently, and they labored on…and on…and on. When they finally finished, it was nearly dark, but I heard Bill compliment Eddy for a job well done.

The next day, we took a day trip north to Koma and Malberg, where I was pleased to see the boulder that has occupied that spot by the waterfall at the end of the portage for ten thousand years. This year, only a trickle of water was flowing through the rocks of the streambed, so different from the frothy flow of past years. As we paddled across the lake, we played a game in which Eddy was a humanoid who needed to have his solar cells charged with sunlight. When I held my paddle between him and the sun, his speech slowed and gradually came to a stop mid-sentence. Then I moved my paddle. Illuminated, he was instantly animated. His antics reminded me of how I feel before and after my first cup of morning coffee.

As we pulled into shore at the campsite on the narrows of the northeast arm of Malberg, Eddy hooked a good-sized northern. We were all delighted. Then, after lunch, Eddy and I went out fishing while Jim stayed on shore. As we were paddling back toward Jim, Eddy spotted a small bear, probably a large cub, standing on the shore. The bear looked in our direction and then slipped into the water, swam across the channel and exited near where Jim was standing. We paddled hard to Jim, and he clambered in.

The next morning, while we were sitting by the shore eating Bill's pancake breakfast, a mother, father and two young children in two green Old Town canoes passed by our campsite. They were paddling in the direction of the Lady Chain portage. We asked where they were heading, and they said they would probably stop for lunch on Hazel, where they had camped last year in a spectacular thunderstorm, and then head on. The father, who was wearing a "Save the Coast" T-shirt, told us that fish the size of our arms were lined up and waiting for us.

"Those would be too small for us," Dad said.

Later, as we paddled down the narrow channel and the steep banks of the Knight River, Jim said it felt like we were penetrating deeper into the wilderness. I love that feeling. The farther I travel from civilization, the more real everything seems. When we arrived on Hazel, we found that once again the lake was ours, and as we generally do on Hazel, we spent two days there. That night after dinner, our fireside conversation was interrupted by a choir of loons singing their otherworldly harmonies.

I'M SITTING ON my favorite campsite on my favorite lake in the Boundary Waters wilderness. Dad is snoring in his tent. Our outpost, our home in the wilderness. The half moon, burnt orange, has risen above the treetops on the eastern shoreline. Eddy thinks he saw a wolverine earlier today and is excited about seeing another. Unfortunately, the loon that was fishing the lake earlier today took off, making a long run across the lake, stepping all the way. It circled twice and then flew off over the tree line in the direction of Knight Lake. I was hoping it would stay and serenade us through the night. The plan is to get up early in the morning to look for moose around the lake. Jim wants to sit in the woods away from any trails and see what comes by. He calls it a "stakeout."

Earlier today, as we were paddling back from the campsite on the southeastern shore, Eddy compared our progress to cutting glass with a diamond. He seemed proud of his metaphor and looked back to me for approval. I told him I liked it. I, too, was proud.

One side of me is hot from the fire, the other chilled from the night air. If it weren't against the rules, I might build a second fire the way the Indians did and sit between them.

The moon has gone from orange to white as it has climbed higher in the sky. Earlier, when the flame of its light first caught my eye, I thought the woods were on fire before I realized it was the moon.

I stand up and stretch, then walk over to Eddy's lookout tree. I close my eyes, and the years roll by. Once, when I was little, I sat high atop a bendy tree with my younger brother, Tim. I had nailed a single wood plank between two branches and called it a tree house. We were so high up that we swayed wildly in the wind. Tim grabbed onto the branch and held on for dear life, but I thought it was a great ride. I felt like I was floating in space.

Today, I began carving a ball-in-a-box for Eddy, like the ones my scoutmaster Mac used to make at summer camp. I'm carving it from a little chunk of red cedar. At this point, it's nothing more than a rectangular box, but I'm working on the four columns. Eventually, I'll carve the middle part into a little ball that will roll free of its supports. If all goes well, I'll get the dimensions right, and the ball won't fall out. As I worked on it, I would hold it to my nose and sniff its sweet cedar scent.

The wind is stirring the pines. These starlit nights, even with the competing light from the moon, lead invariably to thoughts of the origins of the universe, creation and our place in it. To think that Voyager 2 is now taking photos of Neptune's largest moon, Triton, and that NASA hopes to spend about $100 million over the next ten years on Project SETI, the Search for Extraterrestrial Intelligence. I wonder if they'll find anything. If they do, I hope the discovery will remind us that we earthlings are all related and as brothers and sisters we should stop our fighting.

The moon, now high in the sky, is casting its dreamy white light on the open space of our campsite. The tents are partly illuminated by its light and partly shadowed by the pines. I hear a dull thud. There it is again. It's my canoe bumping against the rocks. I'll beach it before I turn in. Should have done that already.

The fire is nearly out, its yellow flames fading to a red glow. I'll sleep well tonight. I wish the loon had stayed. I close my eyes. With just the suggestion of heat from the dying fire, I think of how that loon had disappeared beneath the water and then reappeared, opening its wings. It held them above its body in what looked like a comfortable stretch and then shook its tail, its body and finally its beak. A moment later, it lifted one broad, webbed foot out of the water and held it in the air to soak up the sun's heat. Loon magic. I hope to watch this movie many more times before I die.

In *Love of Loons*, Kate Crowley and Mike Link tell a story about a loon attacking some mallard chicks and another about a confrontation between a loon and a beaver. I especially like the Tsimshian Inuit legend they describe. Here's how it goes: An old man had gone blind, and his heart was "breaking with grief" because he could no longer hunt to support his wife and son. He was standing on the shore, singing his sad song, when a loon heard it and replied with its own sad song. Swimming near the old man, the loon asked if it could help. The old man offered "his prize possession, a shell necklace," if the loon could restore his sight. Telling the man to hold onto its wings and "bury his eyes in its feathers," the loon dove twice. The first time it surfaced, the man "could see the shape of trees." The second time, he "had regained his full vision." Overjoyed, the man tossed his necklace to the loon, which fell onto the loon's black feathers and around its neck. And that's how the loon got its white necklace.

Earlier today, I heard a noise like a soft mew. It came from overhead. I was stretched out on my back, dozing beneath a pine. In the lowest branch, only five feet from my head, were two Canada jays looking down at me. One was leaning so far forward that I thought it might tumble head over heels onto my belly. In *Canoe Country*, Jaques describes her own encounter with these curious creatures:

> *Now, as we sat in our cave, sheltered from the strong gusts, a whole family of moose birds gathered around us, looking at us with friendly eyes, cocking their black-capped heads inquisitively. This fluffy gray bird is a jay, the Canada jay, also called the camp robber and whisky jack, the last derived from his Indian name, Wis-ka-tjon. He seems to have no fear of man at all, though he chooses to live in the wild woods instead of around settlements. I had been wanting to see a moose bird, having heard so many tales of his brazenness and robberies. But I decided today that he is misjudged. Crows are crafty and clever thieves, taking an ironic pride in the knavery. But the moose bird is so wide-eyed and innocent—I can't quite believe he thinks he is a robber at all; he just borrows things, feeling sure you won't mind, since he is a friend of yours.*

Their boldness does make them seem friendly, but I wonder how friendly they really are. I know how nature works. If I had been dead rather than half asleep, I doubt they would have been content with merely taking a good look at me before flying off. I'm guessing they would have started with my eyes.

Nature is good, as Dad's friend Bill is fond of saying, but it isn't kind. Every creature out here does what it needs to do to survive. I'm amazed by the complex and sophisticated ways plants and animals have evolved to meet their basic needs. In *Boundary Waters Canoe Area Wilderness*, Kate Crowley and Mike Link describe how a plant with the deceptively nice name of "sundew" goes about its business:

> [The leaves] *are shaped like spoons or spatulas with short, translucent hairs. Each hair exudes a droplet of "dew," which is sweet tasting and sticky. An insect with an attraction to sweets soon finds itself stuck on its lunch and struggles to get free. The struggle is useless, except that the vibrations stimulate a hormone release that causes the outside half of the hairs to grow rapidly. Since the tension of the nongrowing half is toward the center of the leaf, the hair bends inward and the insect is caught in a closed cage. An enzyme is released that dissolves the insect's soft tissues, and the plant feeds. Then, with the new nitrogen, the plant releases a second hormone that causes the insides of the hair to grow to a matching length, straightening out the plant hairs and ejecting the exoskeletal remains of the insect.*

Amazing, but hardly friendly or kind.

I place one more piece of split wood on the fire, and it crackles in yellow flames. Such a lovely sound. The wind stirring the pines overhead makes me feel uneasy, but the sound of the fire is comforting. Maybe there's something to Sig's notion of "racial memory," of things ingrained into our collective consciousness from thousands and thousands of years of experience.

Yesterday, I found a rusty, bent spike at the end of one of our portages, a remnant from an old pier. I was tempted to keep it as a souvenir, but I left it where it belonged. Removed from its environment, it would have lost its allure and authenticity.

Earlier tonight, at twilight, Bill and I went for a paddle. We marveled at the lingering light in the northwestern sky. "It's as though it gets brighter," Bill said. I've noticed the same thing. After the sun sets, the light shifts to the north, creating a second light, one with a peculiar quality. It's peaceful, quiet, enchanting.

When we returned to camp, Bill made some popcorn. While we were eating it, Jim mentioned the alligator dance we used to do at fraternity parties at Vanderbilt. He teased Eddy by talking about it without actually describing it. As I remember it, the alligator dance was nothing more than lying on the floor on your back and flailing about with your arms and legs. It had seemed pretty wild in our southern campus environment, but as I picture it now it seems pretty ridiculous. I wonder how Eddy imagines the scene. I suspect his version is more interesting than the reality.

A mouse darts into and out of the light at my foot. Unlike Bill, I make no attempt to stomp on it. I am, however, watching for it out of the corner of my eye. Earlier, Bill asked if I thought Debbie would enjoy a canoe trip. She certainly wouldn't enjoy the mice. Or the bats flitting across the water and swooping near her head. One of these years, I hope to talk Kate into coming.

I hear a whisper. What was it? Maybe the whoosh of expanding air escaping from that last log in the fire. Night sounds.

Hup! That one made me jump. It was a sudden, unfamiliar sound. I get up to investigate. It was our plastic drink carton stirred by the wind. I tuck it beneath a tarp.

Today, I heard chickadees back in the woods and saw a gull on the lake. On our moose hunt, the three boys—Eddy, plus the two older boys, Jim and me—took the 144-rod portage to Knight for a look around. Then we hiked cross-country to the north portage of Hazel, Jim's idea. He wanted to get off the main travel route and back into the woods. One of the nice things about traveling with different people in the wilderness is that each person brings his own ideas of fun things to do. On our expedition, we discovered that the woods were crisscrossed by animal trails, and we saw piles of moose turds. We also saw lots of tracks, mostly moose but some from a small animal, maybe a fox. In places, the thick undergrowth was nearly impassable. Without the portage trails, I realized, hiking cross-country in this terrain would be nearly impossible. We climbed up and down both sides of the rocky stream bed that leads down the river, which was nearly dry this year.

Late in the day, a family of four in two canoes passed by on the lake. Their appearance made us feel as though we had lost our solitude, but after they disappeared, our sense of aloneness soon returned. I love this campsite. I love them all, but especially this one. When was the last time I was here with Eddy and Dad? Let's see. According to my journal, it was three years ago, in 1986, Eddy's third trip.

THE NEXT DAY, Jim, Eddy and I did our stakeout in the woods. We were surprised by something literally beneath our feet. Jim uncovered it when he leaned his backside against a moss-covered rock and then dug in his heel to push himself up and sit down. As he did, out flipped a chunk of moss, and there, nestled in the opening, was a toad. It was like opening a can and finding a toad inside. When Eddy patted it on the head and rubbed it under the chin, it closed its eyes. Though no expert on toad expressions, I thought this one looked supremely content. Before leaving, we popped the moss back in place, closing the door to the toad's comfy little home.

Back at camp, Eddy climbed thirty feet up the two tall jack pines near the fire grate. Then he teased Bill by winging pinecones and pieces of bark at him. He was encouraged by Bill's hearty laugh and undeterred by his threats of vengeance.

In the morning, as we pulled away from our Hazel campsite, Dad grabbed our stern for a free ride. When I noticed the extra drag, we had a good laugh. The sky stayed clear until we got to Phoebe, where a bank of low steam clouds moved toward us across the lake, enshrouding the tops of the hills on the east shore. Jim said it felt like we were in the mountains. I was just about to reach for my rain suit when, as quickly as the clouds had appeared, they vanished—or maybe we paddled out from under them when we turned east. The last portage from Grace to Beth was a long one, 287 rods. It was hilly, with a beaver meadow on one side. Beautiful.

On Beth, we were delighted to find that the campsite near the jumping rock, the one on the east end of the lake where I had served dinner to Dad and Eddy in the tent, was open. At first, the site didn't look right. Then I

A pinecone attack from above unchecked by threats of vengeance.

realized what was different. The smooth wet gray rock where I had stood in the rain was now a warm, inviting sun terrace.

Unlike Hazel, which is an *unexceptionally* beautiful Boundary Waters lake, Beth is an *exceptionally* beautiful Boundary Waters lake. Its surrounding hills, necklace of pink granite boulders, clear water, small islands and mature stands of white and red pine give it a distinctive character. To have this lake, so near to the entry point, all to ourselves felt like a bonus at the end of a good trip. Here and there along the shore, maple saplings had turned a brilliant red, harbingers of the season to come. This had been one of our cooler trips, although every day except Sunday had been sunny for at least part of the day. After dinner, Dad and Bill went out for a paddle while the three youngsters hiked the rugged terrain between our campsite and the portage.

On our way out the next day, we spotted a pileated woodpecker on a dead tree. Then, just as we were coming around the point to the portage leading from Alton to Sawbill, we saw three American bald eagles. I heard their whistles before I saw them. At first we thought the juvenile was a golden eagle. Eddy spotted the nest. As we paddled away from its territory, one of the parents monitored our movement with fierce eyes.

8

One Honkin' Lake Trout, Spectacular Northern Lights and Summer's End on Flame Lake

I hear a loon wailing in the distance. Haunting. Unspeakably wild. The sound carries a kind of wisdom. John Muir was right. The cry of the loon authenticates the North Woods.

There are five of us this year: Dad, Bill, Eddy and me, along with Sam, a friend of Dad and Bill's from work. It's good to be sharing a tent with Dad again. I'm sitting by the fire writing. We're on the east-shore campsite on the north end of Sawbill Lake, down from the campsite where the bear walked up to Eddy on his second trip in 1985. The last time I camped here was the trip Dad and I canoed alone in 1982, eight years ago. It's good to be back.

By the time Eddy and I arrived at the end of the Sawbill Trail, it was nearly dark. Dad, Bill and Sam were making the twenty-one-hour drive from Cincinnati and wouldn't arrive until the next day. Eddy and I had planned to pitch a tent in the campground, but instead we decided to sleep in the car in the Sawbill parking lot. Before turning off my flashlight, I read to Eddy from Gary Paulsen's *The Winter Room.* When I got to the episode where Wayne jumps from the hayloft to his horse in imitation of a Zane Grey cowboy—misses his horse, lands on the ground and calls, "I'll be back with the posse"—Eddy started laughing his big belly laugh.

This morning, as we set off in the canoe paddling north on Sawbill Lake, with Dad in the bow and Eddy duffing in the middle, I felt a rush of memories and good feelings. Once again, I was in my beloved canoe country. As we paddled past the point with the BWCAW sign, Eddy turned to me and said, "I'll be back with the posse." The older guys wondered why we were laughing so hard.

The only mishaps so far are Eddy's leaving his short paddle at the Sawbill landing (we were just north of the portage to Smoke when I realized it was missing) and Dad's forgetting to pack the dishwashing supplies, but it was only a half-hour round trip to retrieve the paddle, and we're using soap shavings for cleanup.

It seems like an easy-going group. Sam fits right in. He reminds me of Bill—a straightforward kind of guy, although he speaks with more bluster than Bill. He seems proud of all the books he's read, and he likes mentioning titles and asking me if I've read them. He's also a dedicated body-builder. He's short but has huge biceps and a barrel chest. To Bill's surprise and chagrin, however, when it comes to paddling, he's "a dipper." When Bill grew impatient over the lack of power in the front of the canoe, he suggested they switch positions, only to discover that Sam had trouble learning the J-stroke and couldn't get the knack of steering. As they zigzagged across the lake, they fell even farther behind. At the next portage, they switched back to their original positions, with Sam in the bow and Bill in the stern, and they made faster progress.

Tonight, after dinner, as we were sitting around the campfire, Dad told me it was hard to hear what I was reading from the other tent last year, so I read from Paulsen to the entire group. Afterward, I took a paddle before turning in. From the lake, I could see the yellow light of our campfire and the light of another campfire just north of us. The stars were brilliant, and the Milky Way extended like white smoke from the North Star all the way down to the tree line on the south horizon.

In the morning, we woke to a clear, nearly cloudless day, warm in the sun and cool in the shade—my favorite kind of Boundary Waters day. As is his habit, Bill got up first, started the fire and had hot coffee waiting. As I sat sipping my coffee and breathing the fresh morning air, two seagulls kept watch over us. It's a pretty campsite, with a big pine right on the water's edge and our tent not more than eight feet from the water.

For the first time this early on a trip, we single-portaged when we took the four portages from Sawbill to Cherokee—that is, we carried all of our equipment in a single trip rather than doubling back. "The difference is Eddy," Bill said. Eddy, now eleven years old, carried Dad's big red pack on his back, his small pack on his front, plus the fishing poles, night crawlers and the empty plastic water jug. Because the lakes are low again this year, we had

A heap of equipment just waiting to be loaded and portaged.

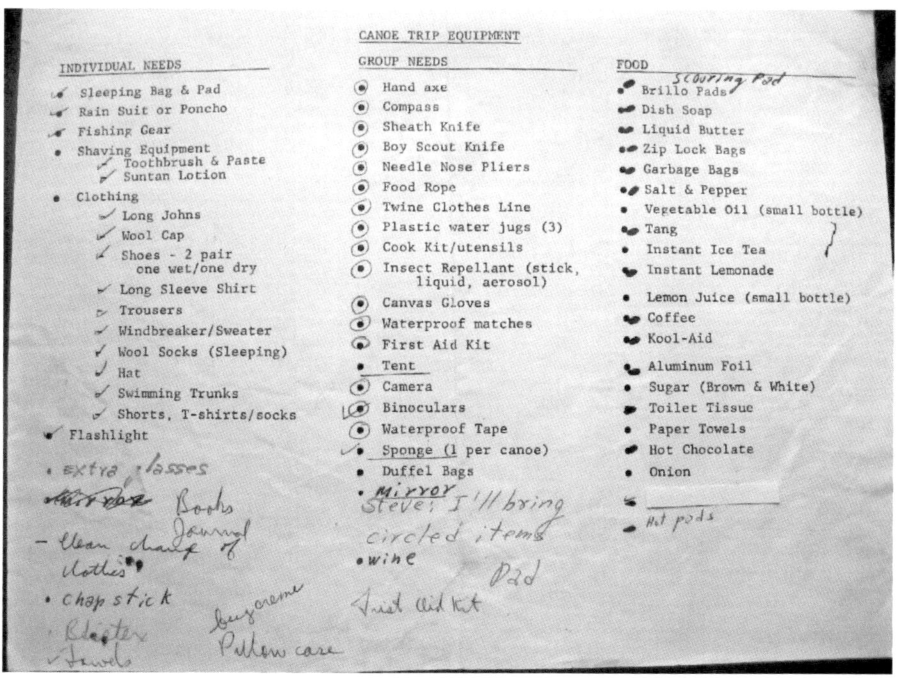

CANOE TRIP EQUIPMENT

INDIVIDUAL NEEDS
- Sleeping Bag & Pad
- Rain Suit or Poncho
- Fishing Gear
- Shaving Equipment
  - Toothbrush & Paste
  - Suntan Lotion
- Clothing
  - Long Johns
  - Wool Cap
  - Shoes - 2 pair one wet/one dry
  - Long Sleeve Shirt
  - Trousers
  - Windbreaker/Sweater
  - Wool Socks (Sleeping)
  - Hat
  - Swimming Trunks
  - Shorts, T-shirts/socks
- Flashlight
- extra glasses
- Books
- Journal
- clean change of clothes
- chap stick
- bug creme
- Pillow case

GROUP NEEDS
- Hand axe
- Compass
- Sheath Knife
- Boy Scout Knife
- Needle Nose Pliers
- Food Rope
- Twine Clothes Line
- Plastic water jugs (3)
- Cook Kit/utensils
- Insect Repellant (stick, liquid, aerosol)
- Canvas Gloves
- Waterproof matches
- First Aid Kit
- Tent
- Camera
- Binoculars
- Waterproof Tape
- Sponge (1 per canoe)
- Duffel Bags
- Mirror
- wine
- First Aid Kit

Steve: I'll bring circled items

Dad

FOOD
- Brillo Pads / Scouring Pad
- Dish Soap
- Liquid Butter
- Zip Lock Bags
- Garbage Bags
- Salt & Pepper
- Vegetable Oil (small bottle)
- Tang
- Instant Ice Tea
- Instant Lemonade
- Lemon Juice (small bottle)
- Coffee
- Kool-Aid
- Aluminum Foil
- Sugar (Brown & White)
- Toilet Tissue
- Paper Towels
- Hot Chocolate
- Onion
- Hot pads

A late 1980s wilderness canoeing packing list.

to push the canoes free with our paddles several times in the shallow stream leading into Ada, where I spotted the little island with the steep rock ledge. Five years have passed since Dad rescued Eddy.

The 180-rod portage into Cherokee, the last of the four, seemed interminable. At about the halfway point, a dozen trees were down, all laid out in the same direction, apparently toppled by a straight-line windstorm. For lunch, we stopped on the campsite on the west shore of Cherokee, where Eddy spotted a river otter. It was the first time we had ever seen one. We watched it swim to shore and scamper up a rock point. Its exuberant antics were a delight to watch. Today, Eddy asked if we were going to camp on any small lakes, where we would have a better chance of seeing beaver. He knows the Boundary Waters wilderness well.

From our lunch site, we headed north to the campsite on the west end of the long narrow island about midway in the lake. Although we were put off by how open and worn the campsite was behind the rock point, where the fire grate is located, we were delighted with the view, so we stayed, swam, bathed and loafed.

Before dinner, Eddy and I went fishing. We paddled north past Mouse Island, where we threw in our lines and discovered a deep hole near a rock cliff by the east shore. Suddenly, Eddy's pole bent double. "I think you hooked a big one," I said. As he tried to reel in, the fish dove and took out line. Finally, Eddy brought it into the canoe. It was a gorgeous lake trout that had fought him all the way. It must have weighed four pounds, maybe eight. The first thing Eddy said when we landed his prize was: "I know how to mount the head!" He had read an article with instructions in *Boy's Life.*

Back at camp, the older men marveled at Eddy's catch. After Bill cleaned it, Sam stuck the fish head on the end of a stick and paraded down the path like one of the boys in *Lord of the Flies.* Eddy was thrilled. The thought of carrying a rotting fish head with us on the rest of the trip, however, didn't appeal to me, so I talked Eddy out of keeping it. He was disappointed, but he cheered up as we ate his fish for dinner. Everyone complimented him on his fine catch.

As always on these trips, the loons and their calls have delighted us. On a single day, we saw two pairs and one family of four, a good sign for the health of their population. On another day, we heard several hooting to one another as they fished. Then a male did his territorial yodel, and three loons tremoloed as they flew overhead. Toward evening, we heard a chorus of wails. With that, we had heard all four of their sounds: the hoot, the yodel, the tremolo and the wail. In *The Boundary Waters Wilderness Ecosystem*, Bud

"I think you hooked a big one."

Heinselman describes some of their "complex repertoire of vocalizations":

> *Hoots are short soft notes among loons close to each other, apparently used to keep in touch. Wails are the long, mournful calls that sometimes sound almost like wolf howls. Pairs also use wails to get together when separated, and males use them to lure the female to shore for mating. Most calling occurs at night, tending to peak just before midnight. Tremolos are "laughing" calls, given in three variations involving frequency changes. On the water tremolos are alarm calls; the higher the frequency the more likely the bird will leave (often underwater).*

With the memory of their calls reverberating in my head, I switched off my light, rolled over in my sleeping bag and closed my eyes. It had been quite a day.

THE NEXT DAY was equally gorgeous. Once again, it was nearly cloudless and cool but warm in the sun. Our string of great weather was unbroken.

We took a day trip to Gordon Lake, where we were impressed by its hilly shoreline, sheer rock walls and beautiful mature white pines on the north end of the lake. I noticed many dead balsam trees covered with gray-green moss. From the round holes bored into the trunks, we wondered if they were victims of some kind of insect invasion or if we were seeing woodpecker holes made after the trees had been killed by spruce budworm. According to Bill Hansen's map, spruce budworm invasions are a natural phenomenon that occurs every fifty years or so. "Until modern times," Bill explains, "it was a major precursor to wild fire."

I caught a nice northern, and then we paddled over to the flat rock wall to the east of the portage, where Eddy snagged the jig he had used to catch his lake trout. After circling and pulling his line from every direction, I realized it was caught fast, so I gave it the do-or-die tug, and his line snapped. He tried not to cry, but he hates losing his fishing tackle, especially a favorite jig. With a few big tears rolling down his cheek, he said he didn't want to fish anymore. I tied a leader and spinner on his line and threw it back in, hoping for a fish to help him shake his disappointment. As luck would have it, I got a strike and handed the pole to him. "Bring it in!" I said. It was another northern, bigger than the first. I swooshed at it with the net, but it dove and I missed it. Then it jumped and spit out the lure, which spun and hooked it in the head. I took a second swipe with the net, and this time I got it. Laughing, we agreed it was a novel way to land a fish. After we released it, Eddy said he wanted to keep fishing.

Back on Cherokee, we explored the jumping rock island just south of Mouse Island, the same one our large group had explored two years earlier. Then we climbed the larger bluff on the east end of the island where we were camped. This one was way up there, maybe thirty feet, much more of a commitment—and a risk—than the other jumping rock. We were tempted to give it a try but decided not to. It was one thing to take a chance at home, but out here in the wilderness, far from medical care, it was better to err on the side of caution. Things can happen.

As they did earlier in the summer. A six-year-old boy from Shakopee disappeared while canoeing with a church group. Twelve-member teams and a helicopter searched the area to no avail, fearing he had gone over a seventy-five-foot waterfall and through a set of rapids in the Basswood River. He disappeared as the members of his group were unloading their canoes and walking toward their campsite. As reported in the *Minneapolis Star Tribune*, he had asked to take off his life jacket. "I figured he was behind me," his mother said. "When we set the canoe down and looked around, he was gone." It was unlike the boy to venture near the water. "I don't know what we're going to do next," his mother said. "He was warned to stay away from the waterfalls and the rapids. He knew what rapids were about. He was afraid of them." It was a parent's worst nightmare. "Later that evening," the paper reported, "his shoe was found floating in the river near the area where his mother first noticed he was gone."

Wilderness canoeing involves risk. To ignore risk would be foolish. But to deny your child the joy and wonder of the natural world seems equally foolish. Somewhere in the assessment of reasonable risk, even the most responsible parent must factor in the element of chance. Call it what you will—the luck of the draw, fate, God's divine will. Maybe it's nothing more than the cold, uncaring reality of natural law. Whatever the force directing our destinies, on this particular trip a mother and father lost their six-year-old boy through no fault of their own. When Eddy was born, I felt like the luckiest man in the world. What if something had happened to my boy on his first trip, when he was four? Would Debbie have forgiven me? Would I have forgiven myself? Maybe not, but I'm glad we took the risk.

Fortunately, most scary situations and close calls in the wilderness have happy endings. There was another story in the *Minneapolis Star Tribune* about a woman who went into labor at three o'clock in the morning. She was seven weeks before her due date. By five-thirty, her contractions were five minutes apart. Her partner "wrapped her in a sleeping bag, took down the tent, and loaded the canoe." As many canoeists have learned, when the unexpected happens, you do what you have to do. "I'd paddle," the woman said, "then stop, and lean back for a while when I had a contraction." Her partner said, "It was stroke, stroke, stroke. Then I'd yell from the stern, 'Breathe, breathe, breathe.'"

In the hour and half it took them to reach their truck, the woman paddled away, with no complaints. "She even helped load the canoe on the truck," her partner said. "What a frontierswoman." As they neared Duluth, the contractions were only three minutes apart. Their premature baby boy weighed just over four pounds. He was born forty-one minutes after they arrived at the hospital. Although he would have to spend some time in the neonatal unit, both mother and son were fine. "It was an enchanted Boundary Waters experience," said the father. "If anybody has a hard time with labor, I'd say a canoe trip is the way to go." I wonder if the mother would agree.

Back on our campsite, I settled in by the fire for some quiet time after everyone else had gone to bed. It had been a great day, and I wanted to be alone with my thoughts. When I looked up, I couldn't believe what I was seeing. I hesitated, but only for a moment, and then I ran to the tents.

"Wake up! Wake up!" I said, trying to keep my voice down. "You won't believe this!"

"This better be good," Dad said, as he climbed out of his tent.

Covering the entire sky, from horizon to horizon in all directions, were undulating curtains of dancing, shimmering flames. Their light was eerie and unnaturally bright. Oddly, the peak of the pulsing dome slanted south rather than north. We now appreciated the openness of our campsite. There were occasional exclamations of "Unbelievable!" and "Extraordinary!" and "I've never seen anything like it!" alternating with hushed silence. As I watched in fascination, something stirred within me—awe, wonder, reverence, but also unease. It felt as though I was witnessing something beyond our natural world. Then, just when we thought the show could be no more spectacular, the lights intensified into bright white spots whose reflections were clearly visible in the lake, the lower parts rimmed with red. After a long while, they dimmed, but only slightly, and chilled by the night air, everyone headed back to their tents.

"Thanks," Dad said as he zipped the tent closed behind him. "That was worth it."

Lifting one end of the canoe, careful not to let it bang on the rock, I turned it right side up and eased it into the water. I hadn't made a sound. Then I paddled out to the open part of the lake south of the island, where I sat for a long time watching the heavenly display, the aurora borealis, thinking about life and our place in the universe, thinking about my family and friends, feeling fortunate to have this time with my father and my son. Above me, the northern lights flashed in the sky, silent fireworks exploding like puffs of steam above the dark shoreline.

The next day, we traveled to South Temperance and camped on the east campsite near the Brule portage. I loved its south-facing view of the lake. With its rock ridge, leading from the east entrance and the "back porch" with a view to the west, it was a wonderful site. We last stayed on this site in 1985, when Dad and I talked about his retirement and when Eddy was six years old and on his second trip. After setting up camp, Eddy and I swam the narrow channel to the small island just off the campsite. Later that afternoon, I showed Eddy my "secret path," which led to an enclosed space in the trees, but he had already discovered it on his own. He called it "the prison." Funny, I had thought of it more as a sanctuary.

Sam caught his first fish in the afternoon. He wasn't about to give up until he had. Now I hoped both Dad and Bill would land one. After dinner, Eddy and I went out. We let the canoe drift to the cove and campsite on the northwest part of the lake and then paddled counterclockwise around the large island. We met Dad and Bill coming the other way. As the canoes passed each other, Dad asked if we had any news from the rest of the world. Later, Eddy and I came close to two loons, who tremoloed for their chick, which we hadn't seen until it scurried across the water to them, its head low as though it were trying to scoot unseen beneath our line of vision. As they reunited, the adults hooted, the chick made little squeaking sounds and the three of them swam off together.

Then we paddled into a little cove on the west end of the island, with the setting sun casting its light on the rocks and cedars along the shoreline. I love the golden green radiance of cedars drenched in the sun. The light captures the feel of a late summer day. The cove was a cozy and comforting spot. On the other side of the island, we encountered two beavers, an adult and a juvenile, squeaking constantly at each other as they stripped the bark from two aspen branches in rapid little bites. The adult swam toward us to challenge us and then turned and slapped its tail before diving. Before slipping beneath the surface, the youngster gulped a few last bites. I guess there's no suppressing a juvenile's appetite.

We've seen no wolves, eagles or moose yet this trip, but it was a good day for wildlife. As I sat on the biffy, a wonderful location for communing with nature, a little yellow and olive green warbler came within two feet of me. I watched it daintily and efficiently pick the tiny insects, one stem at a time, from a clump of swamp blue asters, one of the handful of flowering Boundary Waters plants I knew by name. I wished I could name more of the plants found in this region, or even just the plants Bud Heinselman says are found in the riparian habitats:

> *Among the many herbs and ferns often found in the shoreline fringe are royal fern, spearwort, bristly crowfoot, blue flag, grass-leaved goldenrod, white panicled aster, flat-topped white aster, Joe-Pye weed, thoroughwort, swamp-loosestrife, field-mint, mad-dog skullcap, common houstonia, New England blue violet, common bugle-weed, northern ragwort, spotted water-hemlock, dodder, and sundrops.*

Even without Heinselman's knowledge, however, a skilled writer like Jaques is able to describe what she sees with intimate detail and artistry:

The perfect spot for communing with nature.

> *Spreading my array on the bushes to dry, I retreated to the pine shade. Here the moss was soft and brightly green, and I lay full length in it. So I discovered its flowers. Flowers of the moss. I'd like to make a diminutive study of them. Shallow cups of pale green, bright scarlet tips enameled on green stems, tarnished silver discs. Coral dots, tawny seed pods high on slender threads, brown-petaled cups, gold points, rose points, gray-green trumpets. There is a deep gray moss like masses of tiny shrubs, a green velvet that covers stones as smoothly as upholstery, a pale green lichen like minute oak leaves. All these atoms are so sturdy in their miniature loveliness. I want to keep them.*

Names are useful, but they represent only one kind of knowledge. According to Paul Gruchow, names can be "both blessings and curses":

> *On the one hand, they can be—perhaps inevitably are—reductive. A name stands for but does not describe a thing; approached casually or carelessly, the act of naming, therefore, quickly becomes a way of labeling, of categorizing, a substitute for knowing, and every system of categories drifts compulsively toward hierarchy. On the other hand, it is*

impossible for me to imagine knowing something well—much less loving it—without needing to name it. A name is a form of acknowledgment—more than that, of embrace.

We stayed a second day on South Temperance. As we approached the short portage to Brule on a day trip, I remembered the familiar mound of rocks separating the two lakes and the pool of dark, still water on the South Temperance side, a peaceful setting that invites you to linger. On Brule we paddled to the east tip of the big island and stopped for lunch on the rocky point. I saw a tower on the south shore. I didn't remember having seen it on previous visits, but it must have been there. Was it a fire tower? I made a mental note to ask Bill Hansen. Now, as I looked out over the quiet blue expanse, I found it hard to believe motors were allowed here as recently as 1986, only four years earlier. In response to strong opposition to a motor ban on Brule, an exception had been written into the 1978 Boundary Waters Canoe Area Wilderness Act. The exception allowed motors to be used on Brule until January 1994 or until businesses already in operation in 1977 were terminated. With the closing of the Sky Blue Waters Lodge, the last business on Brule, the motor ban had gone into effect. Since then, use by canoeists on Brule has increased significantly. It's hard for the people who like using motors to be told they may no longer use them, but to me it seemed like a good tradeoff.

With the wind driving the waves into the rocks, Sam sat on the rock shore by the water soaking his ankles, which were so badly sunburned they were swollen. Eddy played with Squeaky, his toad and companion for the trip, and I worked on the cedar ball-in-a-box I had begun carving for Eddy the previous year. With a few slices of my knife, I freed the little block inside the pillars. Now I had to round it into a ball, taking care not to carve off so much wood that the ball would slip through the columns of the box.

After lunch, to avoid the wind, we continued around the island and discovered a tall hill with a huge rock slide of rose granite boulders. Eddy, Bill and I climbed nearly to the top, jumping from rock to rock, intrigued by this dramatic display of geological time. Looking down from on high, we had a sweeping view of the water and forested landscape. We were surprised to see another lake not far from Brule, one that is not visible from water level. What a gorgeous planet, I thought as I looked out over the vista, so bold and delicate in its beauty. What a privilege to inhabit it.

As we were descending, I could smell rain. Clouds were blowing in, ending our streak of carbon-copy cloudless days. By the time we paddled off Brule, it had started to drizzle.

Cold Brule water soothes Sam's sore, sunburned skin.

At the portage to South Temperance, we encountered a group traveling with Wilderness Inquiry. There were three leaders, an able-bodied couple from France and four adults with special needs, two of whom were using lightweight wheelchairs. I enjoyed speaking French with the couple from France. Impressed with how fit Dad was, one of the leaders, a woman, complimented Dad on how he could "really throw a canoe around."

Back on our campsite, it started to rain in earnest. By dinner, the rain had lightened to mist, and the sky had turned to solid steel gray. Tomorrow would be our big travel day—five portages to Burnt—so we were hoping for a clear day. I was a little worried about Sam. His left ankle had continued to swell. I hoped he would be all right walking the portages.

Eventually, the mist let up, and we sat by the campfire telling stories. Then Sam and Bill paddled out to the middle of the lake to get water. Cautious canoeists treat, filter or boil their water to avoid contracting giardia, a parasite carried by beaver that can cause fever, abdominal bloating, nausea and diarrhea in humans. But for us, one of the pleasures of being in the Boundary Waters wilderness is drinking the water straight from the lake, as one would be able to anywhere on an unspoiled planet.

We do, however, take the precaution of fetching our water well away from shore, where the lake is deep and beavers are less likely to have defecated. I once asked Bill Hansen whether the water was safe to drink, and he told me he recommended to his customers that they treat or filter it. Then I asked him if he himself treated the water or drank it straight from the lake, and he said he and his crew members all drank it straight from the lake.

On our last full day in the Boundary Waters wilderness, we paddled under an overcast sky with no wind and smooth water. We did well paddling and portaging from South Temperance to Weird and then traveled on to Jack with its beds of wild rice, to Kelly and finally to Burnt with its green algae-stained water, with Eddy double-packing all the way.

Though tired, Bill and I were eager to see Flame, a little lake with one portage leading in and none leading out. Travelers might visit Flame just to see it or they might go there to camp, but they don't travel through it, so it tends not to have much traffic. We talked it over with Dad and Sam and agreed that Bill, Eddy and I would paddle and portage to Flame to see if the single campsite on the lake was open while Dad and Sam held the campsite on Burnt. As we arrived at the end of the portage to Flame, the sun broke through the clouds. The lake was beautiful, with a rock bluff across the water from the campsite. We loved its cozy, isolated feel. We paddled over to the campsite and were delighted to find it open, so we left a pack on it and headed back to deliver the good news to Dad and Sam. By the time we paddled back to the campsite on south Burnt, however, they had started gathering wood and making camp. They were annoyed with us for leaving the pack and committing us to moving on, and we were annoyed with them for beginning to make camp while we were checking out a site. After a few cross words, we paddled to Flame.

After we had pitched our tent, I invited Eddy to go for a paddle. This trip was his seventh, the thirteenth for Dad and me. The photos show Eddy's get-up—jeans with holes in the knees, wolf sweatshirt, Boundary Waters cap, sunglasses on a cord and a slingshot and hunting knife slung from his waist—a man of the woods, prepared for any eventuality.

After paddling to the center of the lake for water, we headed to the jumping rock by the portage, where we had a nice view of the lake and our campsite. From a distance, all looked tranquil. After I had checked the water depth, Eddy and I clasped hands and jumped off the rock into the dark water. After several more jumps, both solo and tandem, we sat and warmed ourselves in the afternoon sun. We talked and laughed and did imitations

Man of the woods, prepared for any eventuality.

of Molly, our Old English sheepdog, who would cock her head to one side when you talked to her. Then we settled into a peaceful, relaxed silence. I imagined Eddy and I were thinking the same thing. Summer was nearly over, and soon school would start. As we sat looking out across the lake, we could almost feel summer slipping through our fingers.

Back on the campsite, I found a toad and handed it to Eddy. Then I found another and then another, each one bigger than the one before, and I handed those to him as well. Soon, he had four toads squirming in his cap, the last a contribution from his grandpa.

In the tent that night, I heard a light tapping on the nylon. It had started to drizzle. For a long while, it sounded as though it would be no more than a gentle rain. Then it intensified, with flashes of lightning and claps of thunder. Shortly before daylight, the heavens opened, and it poured in a deluge. In the morning, the first words I heard were from Bill, who was standing at the door of our tent. "I think we should just pack up and go," he said. "No breakfast, guys."

Even in our rain suits we were soon soaked. Fortunately, the rain was warm. We managed the three portages to Sawbill nicely, with Dad taking the stern for the last leg. Despite the tension at the end, it had been a good trip.

At the outfitters, Bill Hansen answered my questions: Yes, that was a fire tower southeast of Brule. The rock slide was pink granite. ("Everything up here is granite.") The *critch, critch, critch* sound we kept hearing on our campsites was made by the pine bore, which drills the neat little holes in the trees but only after they're dead. The spruce budworm is what is killing them, not only around Gordon Lake but everywhere in the North Woods. Their presence is a natural occurrence and has been for thousands of years. It explains why there are no mature balsams or spruces in the Boundary Waters wilderness. Eventually, Bill said, they may create a "Yellowstone situation" with a buildup of highly flammable dead wood in the forest. And last, the algae in Burnt Lake is natural, not the result of pollution.

As we drove down the Sawbill Trail, we encountered standing water on the road. A couple vehicles were pulled off to the side. A stream was washing across the gravel roadbed. It looked shallow, and the road appeared to be intact, so we drove through it, maybe not a prudent choice, but we made it over without incident.

As we continued down the Sawbill Trail, I knew I would remember this trip for those first four gorgeous days, the spectacular northern lights on Cherokee, Eddy's huge lake trout, the waves beating against the rocky point at our lunch spot on Brule, our teasing Sam about leaving an impression of his butt where he had sat on the rock shore, the Wilderness Inquiry group, the tension toward the end and those precious moments on Flame Lake when I sat with my son on the rock cliff in the late afternoon sun and we could feel summer slipping through our fingers.

9

Wolves Howling, Beavers Cooing and Boys Chattering

We're relaxing on the rock ledge overlooking the channel. The year is 1991. Eddy, now twelve, and his red-haired, freckle-faced friend Nick have their lines in the water. Dad and Bill are having a conversation over wine. I'm writing in my journal. We're camped on the first campsite east of the portage from Townline, a gorgeous campsite. Dad remembered seeing it on previous trips when it was occupied. We hoped we could camp there one day, and now here we are. The cool breeze feels good on our skin and tired muscles. The sun is sparkling on the water. The air is fresh and sweet. Except for the murmur of the men's voices and the occasional exclamations from the boys, it's quiet.

I love the way you open yourself up to your surroundings in the Boundary Waters wilderness. In urban areas, with the racket from planes and traffic and lawnmowers and leaf blowers, your instinct is to block things out. Here, you listen. In the city, you hear noise; in the wild, you hear sounds. As Sig said in that documentary film, "Only when one is silent can one see and understand things that are around you. Without silence and solitude, you cannot understand what this little corner of wilderness is all about."

Earlier today, as we were bobbing in the water, wearing our wet shoes to protect our feet from the rocky shoreline, I said, "This is wonderful."

"Yes," said Bill, "and it wouldn't feel so good if we hadn't worked so hard getting here."

Working hard is an essential part of wilderness canoeing, whether it's paddling a half mile from your entry point to your campsite or paddling for four months and two thousand miles from Le Pas, Manitoba, to Hudson Bay and back, as Ernest Oberholtzer and Billy Magee did in 1912 when they explored an unmapped territory, one that hadn't been visited by a white man since Samuel Hearne traveled through the area in 1770. Working hard is what it's all about, as well as enjoying the journey, opening yourself up to your environment, accepting the risks and—for some people like me—reflecting on your experience by writing things down, as I'm doing now. I'm not sure why, but it's important for me to create a record of our annual trips. Earlier, I thought about what I should call the little blue spiral-bound notebook I write in. "Journal" isn't quite the right word. It's more of a log than a journal. That's it. A log. A Sawbill log.

EDDY, NICK AND I drove from Minneapolis in just over five hours. Dad and Bill flew from Cincinnati in six. The difference in our average speeds was about one hundred miles per hour. After putting our canoes into the water of Kawishiwi Lake, we moved along at about three or four miles per hour.

Eddy and Nick were in my canoe. At first, they flailed away with their paddles. Good, I thought, we would have no problem keeping up with Dad and Bill. Unfortunately, however, the boys' enthusiasm was short-lived. I love paddling, but it was hard work to keep our fully loaded canoe planing on the water and moving at a reasonable pace with little power from the middle and bow.

Tired from our late start, we had planned to camp on Kawasachong, but all four campsites were taken, so we had to push through the 179-rod and 85-rod portages to Polly. By the time we arrived at our campsite, pitched our tents, grilled our steaks and ate our runny pudding, it was early evening, and we were tuckered out, but the clouds and light rain had cleared, the food was good and the evening was beautiful, so our first day turned out fine.

The next day, we had a pleasant lunch break on Koma and then took the portage to Malberg, where I paused by the boulder at the mouth of the stream while Dad and Bill paddled ahead to look for a campsite. The boys ran off with the tent bag, submerged it in the shallow water at the end of the portage and then swooshed it around, trying to capture some minnows. I found a comfortable spot near the boulder, lay back and closed my eyes. Lulled by the sound of the rushing water, I wondered how many times I had passed this stone sentinel. Over the years, it has served as a marker in my life, its solidity and permanence offering me the reassurance of an ordered universe. In *Boundary Waters*, Greg Breining alludes to the odd sense of comfort one feels in the presence of rock:

> *There is something clean and reassuring about rock—and something awesome, too. We lie on an outcrop at night, the rock sucking heat from our bodies, drawing it into the earth. We shift around on the big slab, trying to find contours to accommodate our backs...The life of a rock is a long one, its character slow to change.*

In that 1980 documentary, Sig holds up a piece of greenstone, which he calls "one of the oldest rocks in the world...at least three billion, maybe four billion, years of age," and he says:

> *You find it way up in the far North. This is one of the few places in the world where the greenstone is at the surface. You find it at the bottom of the Grand Canyon. It underlays all the others. But the important thing to us is the tremendous feeling of age. Four billion—that's four thousand million years. It does give you a new dimension as to the significance of time and the relative insignificance of man as he lives close to these ancient formations. It puts one's life into perspective.*

How can one comprehend the vastness of the cosmos? The passage of time would forever remain a mystery to me, although certain writers have helped me achieve an inkling of understanding. In *Basin and Range*, John McPhee offers a helpful illustration of how the span of human history fits into our planet's history. Stand with your arms held out to each side, he says, and let the extent of the earth's history be represented by the distance from the tips of your fingers on your left hand to the tips of the fingers on your right. Now, if someone were to run a file across the fingernail of your right middle finger, then the time that humans have been on the earth would be erased.

The boys' voices roused me from my reverie. I opened my eyes, stretched and sat up. Although they had returned from their hunt for minnows empty-handed, they didn't seem disappointed. In fact, they were laughing so hard they were slaphappy. I told them we should call this spot "Minnow-haha Falls." They liked the idea.

Out on the lake, Dad and Bill were waving their paddles at us. They had found an open campsite on the hillside on the north side of the west channel of Malberg. We were surprised to find ourselves the only campers on the lake, a first for us on Malberg, a hub lake that usually draws a fair number of visitors. That night, with the clouds passing before the nearly full moon, we heard a wilderness sound I love second only to the song of the loon: a pack of wolves howling. I remembered hearing them on Buck's first trip four years earlier. The wolves sounded far away, their howls drifting across the hills north of us from the direction of Kawishiwi River.

Sometime during the night, it started raining, but in the morning as we were cooking breakfast, the clouds cleared to blue sky. While we were eating, we heard beavers cooing from their lodge across the channel. After cleanup, I pushed off in the canoe to inspect, taking the empty water jugs with me. With the breeze pushing me silently toward the lodge on the opposite shore, I heard a soft gurgling that sounded like someone blowing bubbles. A large adult beaver appeared nearby and circled the canoe before ducking under the water with a *ka-thunk.* Naturally, I jumped.

That night, after everyone else was asleep in their tents, I paddled into a little cove, illuminated by the moonlight. The lake was smooth and still, reflecting a perfect image of the silver tree line. The world by moonlight is a magical place, especially when viewed from the water. And part of that magic is the stillness of it. I held my breath so that nothing would interfere with what I was hearing. The silence was total and unbroken, and yet I felt movement all around me, and I sensed an environment teeming with life. In *Cold Comfort: Life at the Top of the Map*, Barton Sutter describes "a kind of luxurious quiet" when traveling by canoe:

> *Such peace is hard to come by these days. The noise of our infernal machinery is nearly omnipresent; clocks and refrigerators hum in our sleep. But the silence of canoe country is more than lack of racket. Silence is not the absence of sound. True silence is spacious and easily includes the splatter of waves, the song of the wind, the jabber of warblers in the high treetops. Sometimes it even seems to contain the glistening yellow of buttercups, the fragrance of wild roses. Silence, as the Quakers know, is never nothing, but a positive force, mysterious, sacred, and profound. Out of deep silence, it has always seemed to me, comes the best of what we know—poetry, music, the most moving conversations.*

Some people, I suppose, need noise and commotion to feel alive. Maybe that explains why some, especially men, crave the roar of jet skis, snowmobiles, motorcycles and racecars. Borrowed power and mechanized speed can make you feel strong. Although I understand the thrill of it, I find it more exhilarating to propel myself by my own power. I prefer to paddle a canoe into a stiff headwind with the waves breaking over the bow and then round a point and fly with the breeze or to climb a steep snow-covered hill on Nordic skis and then kick over the top, tuck and go screaming down the other side. What turns me on is using my muscles, asking my body to do what it was made to do. I crave the peace and contentment that comes from working out or pushing myself to my limits. And I love silence. I think it's the most natural thing in the world. As Calvin Rutstrum observes in *Once Upon a Wilderness*, "Most people living in urban centers are so attuned to mechanical noises, the quiet of the wilderness can be initially distressing. This, of course, is a form of neurosis."

The next day, we took a day trip from Malberg to the Kawishiwi River and then to Amber. The day began windy, cloudy and chilly, but the morning sun broke through the clouds, giving way to a gorgeous afternoon. Eddy pulled a large northern right up to the canoe. Unfortunately, we had forgotten our fishing net this year, and as he began to hoist it out of the water, it shook its head and spit out the lure. Nick lunged at it with his bare hands but missed it. Later, as we paddled the narrows, Bill looked down at the white blooms of the water lilies and called them "a perfect flower." On Amber, we were impressed by the long sand beach by the southern campsite and the jumping rock by the northern campsite, where we stopped for a swim. We tried to navigate the stream leading to Bowl to make a loop, but there wasn't enough water for it to be passable. As our canoes bottomed out, we stepped out onto clumps of spongy grass that felt as though they could give way under our weight. Then I realized we were standing on muskeg, that odd formation of vegetative matter and soil that might or might not support your weight. I had first learned about this floating land from Larry on his return from canoeing in Canada with the Boy Scouts. I loved both the idea of floating land and the sound of the word. Muskeg.

Back at the campsite, we were so tired from portaging, swimming and sunning on our "rest day" that no one could stay awake for the first chapter of Jack London's *The Call of the Wild*, which I had brought to read to the boys, both young and old.

The next morning, we were reminded of one of the peculiar things about camping: no matter how carefully you place the plastic bag containing your next meal on top, when you open your pack the next morning it's always on the bottom. It's a phenomenon familiar to every canoeist.

As we were carrying our things down the steep trail of our Malberg campsite, I wondered whether we would make it all the way to Hazel. To my surprise, however, the boys paddled hard, and we arrived in time to eat our sausage-and-cheese lunch at our campsite. The secret to keeping the boys going, I had discovered, was to refer to the middle person as providing "turbo power" to keep ahead of the older guys. "Turbo power" sounded cool, and it motivated the boys to lean into their paddles.

So we made good time, even though Nick left his shoes beside the big rock on the north end of the portage and we had to go back for them. He's a sweet boy, but he can try your patience. He hit Eddy in the head with his paddle four times, fell on the rocks twice and jabbered constantly, but he's fun to have along, and he's good company for Eddy. He also knows a lot about camping, he's not fearful in the woods and he was well packed for the trip—by his mother, who supplied us with a stash of homemade beef jerky. When I told him about a crazed moose that fell in love with a cow and wouldn't leave her side, even when humans approached, he asked, "What did the cow do?"

After lunch, Eddy crawled into the tent for a nap. Hazel has always been a resting place for him. Around mid-afternoon, a red canoe with a lone traveler appeared. He headed for the grassy campsite across the lake, the one with the fallen jack pine on the rock shore. I sat by the shore and carved on Eddy's ball-in-a-box, then shaved and bathed, with Dad pouring sun-warmed pots of water over my head and shoulders. The simplest pleasures are sometimes the best, I thought as I lay back on a narrow rock, warmed by the sun breaking through the clouds in the chill air. Near my head, tiny waves chuckled against the stone shore. If I had rolled over to either side, I would have fallen in.

Rousing myself, I decided to try a few casts from shore. From a rock near the point, I hooked two walleyes, the second large enough to keep for dinner. While the boys made another attempt to catch minnows with the old tent bag, I went out in the canoe with Bill and caught a third walleye, also a keeper. I knew without a net I might lose it, so as I lifted it, I aimed it in the direction of the boat. Sure enough, it spit out the lure just as it cleared the gunwale, landing with a thud and a furious thumping in the bottom of the canoe.

After a delicious walleye dinner, Dad took the lead on cleanup and then reclined in the nook by the jack pine that leans over the lake, the one where Larry liked to sit, and declared it the best seat in the house. I sat down near Dad, and together we took in the view of the lake at dusk. We talked about how his retirement was going, about how he and his partner Joan liked going to Hawaii and Grand Cayman and how he and Joan went out country line dancing nearly every night of the week. When I asked him how many line dances he knew, he said about two hundred. Beyond the overhanging branches, the calm water held the last light of day. There were memories enough here to last a lifetime.

Later, Eddy and I paddled slowly around the lake as the clouds arranged themselves into dark, suggestive shapes around the moon, from time to time obscuring it. After a while, Eddy said, "I think it's quite possible earth is older than scientists think. Maybe mammals lived and died earlier." Later, he said, "Did you know Mount Everest is getting bigger? Scientists measure it each year to see how much it has grown."

On our second day on Hazel, we explored the waterfalls. Eddy had an upset stomach, but he walked along with us anyway, with Nick tripping and falling on the rocks behind us. One rock was like a giant cake sliced into seven pieces. There were three channels in the stream, the deepest tunneling through the streambed at an angle like an underground river. Dad and Bill thought the mossy top of the flat rock above us a perfect place for an Indian chief to call a powwow. I wondered, though, if the rushing water would have made it too noisy.

Back on the campsite, Nick tripped on the low stump between the two tents and yelled in his booming voice, "Who left that there?" His outburst of mock indignation made us laugh. Later, Dad and I paddled across the lake, partly to take a break from the boys' chatter and partly to visit the grassy campsite, recently vacated by the solitary camper in the red canoe. Near one of the tent sites, wild strawberry plants and robust young pines were beginning to reclaim the open space. We marveled at the huge cap of dirt turned up by two trees lying side by side, up-ended by a windstorm. In the fire grate, there was evidence of only the smallest fire, a modest undertaking. In the middle of the gray ashes was a pile of tiny twigs, broken at precisely the same length and meticulously arranged over an even smaller pile of pine needles, ready to be ignited by the match of the next camper. Small. Precisely ordered. Thoughtful. As we launched our canoe, I noticed that the fallen jack pine once held aloft by its broken branches was now a bare trunk lying flat on the rock shore.

That night, with the heat of the glowing campfire warming my skin, I thought about how I was like my older brother, drawing out my time at the end of a trip, trying to make it last as long as possible. Then I heard something stirring in one of the tents, and Eddy called out, "Grandpa. Grandpa!" his voice loud enough to wake Dad.

"What is it, Eddy?" Dad said from the other tent.

I went over to investigate. When I shined my flashlight through the screen of the tent, I saw Eddy sitting up in his sleeping bag. His eyes were closed, and he was mumbling something. Then he said, "Grandpa, look how smooth the rocks are!"

"What?" said Dad.

"Eddy isn't awake," I said. "You're having a conversation with a boy who's asleep."

Dad chuckled and rolled over. I unzipped the flap to Eddy's tent. He didn't wake as I lowered his head and shoulders to the ground.

Back at the fire, I thought of a story from my Boy Scout days about a boy who sleep-walked. Worried he might wander off, his friends would tie a rope around his waist in the tent at night. One night, the boy sat up in his sleep, untied the rope, walked into the lake and drowned.

When I paddled across the lake, there was only the softest of breezes, just enough to counter the power of my stroke and to hold the bow straight without my having to rudder. I turned with the wind and let the canoe drift toward the stream by the portage. At night, there is always that line of shadows close to shore at the base of the trees. Usually, there's enough light from the moon or stars to make out objects farther up on shore, and the contours of the hills are nearly always visible, but that dark band by the water remains shadowy and mysterious. My canoe drifted in the direction of those shadows, and I let it go. When I passed under the overhanging branches and into the darkness, I lost all sense of motion. I knew I was moving, but I could feel no movement, just as I knew the earth moved but could not feel its movement. Suddenly, there was a loud *scritch*, and I jumped. The bow of the canoe had lodged itself against the sharp point of a broken tree branch. I was anticipating the thud of rock against metal, but the scratch of a sharp wooden point had taken me by surprise.

Then I heard something splashing nearby. A beaver? A moose? When I reached for the water with my paddle, I touched rock. With a little shove, I propelled myself backward from shore, weeds rasping along the canoe's metal bottom. Thinking about how ornery a bull moose could be, I felt vulnerable in the shallow water, so I turned and headed away from shore.

I sat for a long time in the middle of the lake, listening to the night sounds, thinking, letting my thoughts drift like my canoe in any direction they wanted to go. Since this morning, when the solitary camper had departed, we have not seen a soul, not even travelers passing through Hazel on their way up or down the Lady Chain. To know we were the only human beings around, perhaps for miles, was a wonderful feeling.

Eddy is murmuring again. The fire is crackling and burning brightly—brighter than I need it to be on this warm night. Think I'll let it burn down. I've been reading entries from earlier trips in my log. What a pleasant way to be reminded of good times.

When I tucked Nick and Eddy into bed tonight, Eddy said, "I love you, Dad." I'm so lucky to be a father. I wonder if I'm teaching him what he needs to learn on these trips. There's more to being a man than knowing how to take care of yourself in the woods, but men still need to teach their boys how to be men. Although I'm not a hunter, I understand the bond that develops between father and child while traipsing through woods and across fields in pursuit of game. And what about Kate? Years ago, a good friend said something I've never forgotten. The most important thing a father could do for a daughter, besides loving her, she said, was to take her seriously. Was I finding ways to connect with Kate as I was with Eddy? Should I have begun taking her canoeing in the Boundary Waters wilderness when *she* was four? From the beginning, our annual canoe trips have been a chance for the guys to spend some time together, as Debbie has encouraged us to think of them, but they don't have to be only for the guys. Maybe I can talk Kate into coming next year.

We made an early start the next day. The narrows of Knight were wild and alluring, and when we arrived on Phoebe we saw a single canoe far across the water, the first people we had seen since the departure of the solitary camper on Hazel. Both campsites were occupied. On Grace, we passed the spot where in 1983 Dad, Eddy and I had come upon a moose carcass in the water. Then we heard something booming in the distance. We thought it might be the sound of blasting—maybe for mining or road work?—but it may have been an approaching thunderstorm. The rain hit us while we were walking the 287-rod portage to Beth. Dad, Bill and I lowered the bows of the two canoes on a canoe rest and huddled under them. The lightning wasn't striking near us, but I was worried about the boys, who had gone on ahead. The moment the downpour passed, we hurried down the portage and found them goofing around at the end of the trail.

After loading the canoes, we paddled out into Beth and, to my delight, found it deserted. Such a gorgeous lake—so various in its beauty after the plainness of Hazel. Once again, we stayed on the campsite near the south portage where I had served the hot dinner to Dad and Eddy in the pouring rain on our 1986 trip. While gathering wood, Dad and

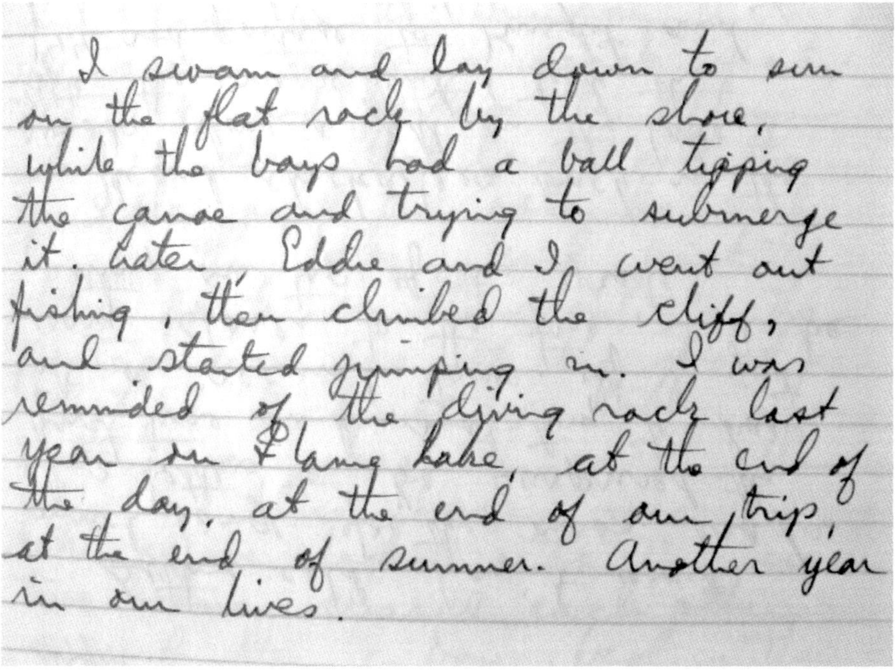
I swam and lay down to sun
on the flat rock by the shore,
while the boys had a ball tipping
the canoe and trying to submerge
it. Later, Eddie and I went out
fishing, then climbed the cliff,
and started jumping in. I was
reminded of the diving rock last
year in Flame Lake, at the end of
the day, at the end of our trip,
at the end of summer. Another year
in our lives.

Remembering the end of the day, at the end of summer.

Bill disturbed a hornet's nest. Dad was stung eight times, Bill once. Fortunately, neither is allergic to bee stings. The boys had a great time tipping the canoe and then trying to submerge it, a fun but impossible task with the built-in flotation in the bow and stern. Later, Eddy and I went fishing, then climbed the cliff by the portage and started jumping in. I was reminded of the diving rock on Flame at the end of the day, the end of our trip, the end of summer. Since that warm, sunny afternoon, another year in our brief lives had passed.

After dinner, our entire group headed back to the rock cliff to watch the sunset. The boys jumped in first. Then Dad, who said he wished he had come over earlier, and then Bill and I. As I was climbing up the rocks for another jump, I saw a stream of water arching from the top of the cliff to the water below. It was Nick peeing into the lake.

"Nick," I yelled. "That's the water we drink!"

He gave me a guilty look and then giggled. I knew he wasn't the only person or animal that would pee in the lake that day, but I was annoyed. Treating the lake like a toilet seemed disrespectful of something I cherished.

That night, as we were sitting around the fire with the last light of day fading from the sky, the wind began stirring and a storm seemed to be brewing, but it never developed. When Dad went down to the shore to beach the canoes, Bill turned to me and said, "Some things you have to leave for your Dad to do," and we laughed. He knows Dad well. They're good company for each other. He's good with all of us. Whenever the boys did or said something typical of boys, I would hear his low chuckle. In the tent, I began reading the last chapter of *The Call of the Wild*, but I stopped four pages short of the ending, just after Buck had killed the bull moose, when I realized both Eddy and Nick had fallen asleep.

The next morning, the last day of our trip, we managed the 144-rod portage from Beth to Alton in good time. As we passed the islands on Alton and then continued up the lake past the three points on the right and turned into the bay to the portage leading to Sawbill, I thought this was one of the most beautiful paddles I had ever taken. The water was absolutely still, blanketed in blue haze as we looked into the sun. Two loons chased each other around the bay, beating their wings and slapping their feet as they went. In the canoe ahead, Dad was wearing his burgundy T-shirt and blue cap, paddling slowly, taking his time, his canoe cutting a perfect V in the still water. Behind us, thunder rumbled, and a line of blue-gray clouds climbed above the horizon. I strained my ears to hear the deep, resonant booming. As with the song of the loons, I could never get enough of the sound of thunder.

At the outfitters, we found Bill in the office. When I mentioned the walleyes in Hazel, he told us they were relatively new. They had been "planted" seven years ago and were doing well, but most people didn't know about them. He described Hazel as a "pass-through" lake for most people because it was too far for a one-day paddle and too close for a two-day trip. Funny, I had always considered it just the right distance for a two-day paddle. He agreed it was a nice place to stop. When I told him how much we enjoyed exploring the stream leading out of the lake, he told us the boulder-lined stream leading into the lake from the east was also worth exploring. We'll have to check it out next time we're there.

As we were loading up the van at the canoe landing, Dad gave Eddy his fishing pole and gear. Eddy was delighted. "Now I won't have to carry it home," Dad said. At the Devil's Track Lake airstrip, Dad let the boys climb into the plane, and he taxied them around the field. At Nick's request, we waited to watch Dad and Bill take off. Next year, the plan was to head up to Long Island Lake from Sawbill and maybe come back through Brule. I was already looking forward to it.

10

THE NATURAL WORLD, AN INTREPID INTRUDER AND STARGAZING WITH YOUR BEST FRIEND

The waves lap against the granite shoreline. I hear laughter in their sound. I can feel myself letting go, the modern world falling away, as I am drawn into a world of natural rhythms and forces.

"Some days are so extraordinary," Calvin Rutstrum writes in *Once Upon a Wilderness*, "they preempt everything utilitarian we planned for them. There is but one thing to do: load the canoe with essentials, start out, and let the events of the day fall where they may." In *Canoe Country*, Florence Page Jaques writes, "What a way to travel—no trains to catch, no traffic to annoy us, no town to reach by evening, no appointments to remember! We wander anywhere our whims take us, through these lakes and rivers."

There are five of us this year, 1992. In addition to Dad, his golfing friend Bill, Eddy and me, there's Jonathan. He has been Eddy's friend since they were in preschool at McRae Park. The two boys, both thirteen, are dressed for effect, decked out in camouflage jackets, pants, hats and nets over their faces. One picture shows them blending into their environment, nearly indistinguishable from the background of trees. They look ready for action and adventure.

Above me, the stars seem both near and far away, their brilliance undiminished by the ambient light of cities and towns. Dad is standing beside me, his head tilted back to the night sky. "So many people never see the Milky Way," he says. "Not once in their entire lives."

OUR FIRST NIGHT out, we camped on the east shore campsite just south of the north bay of Sawbill Lake. On our second day, sunny and warmer than our first, we passed Rescue Rock on Ada and portaged on to Cherokee. After setting up camp on the west end of Mouse Island, we paddled the short distance to Jumping Rock Island and played in the afternoon sun. It rained during the night, and we awoke to steam clouds hovering over the lake, but they soon burned off in the morning sun. On a day trip to Gordon, I picked blueberries with Dad, caught two northerns and helped Eddy pick some leeches from between his toes. Back at our campsite, Eddy boiled and ate three crayfish while Jonathan looked on doubtfully. Eddy offered to share but got no takers.

The next day, we paddled to Frost in a morning rain. It soon cleared, but the wind picked up, pushing rollers and kicking up whitecaps across the lake. We camped on the second site on the rocky point with the sand beach to the north. Frost is like two lakes in one. It has a shallow side and a deep side, with a lone boulder jutting up improbably from the shallow water of the eastern bay. It's "famous for its sand beaches," according to Bill Hansen's map. "Golden sand crescents ring the north end of the lake," he writes, "and you can walk out one hundred yards and be only waist deep. When it does drop off, it goes to about seventy feet and provides good lake trout fishing in the crystal clear depths."

Jonathan, with his relaxed, easy-going personality, is a joy to have along. To make a game of it, he timed himself to see how quickly he could single-handedly set up the tent: "Twenty minutes, thirty seconds," he announced proudly. Dad, Bill and I stayed back on the campsite while the boys hiked out along the sand beach on the north side of our bay, with Eddy in the lead and Jonathan following.

Watching them, I remembered traipsing through the woods with my brothers Larry and Tim and my best friend David. Bill walked up beside me. "There's no place I'd rather be in the world than right here, right now," he said. Later, all five of us headed for the sand beach and walked in the shallow water. As we passed the entrance of two small streams, our feet were washed alternately by clear, icy water flowing from springs and by warmer, amber-colored water flowing from a nearby sun-heated marsh.

That night, we were treated to spectacular northern lights, willowy wisps of green and white, which drew us like a magnet to a flat rock. How many people, I wondered, have marveled at the same sight? "The sky was full of stars," Ernest Oberholtzer wrote in the journal of his 1912 canoe trip with Billy Magee to Hudson Bay (and as quoted by Joe Paddock in his biography of Ober). "Now and then the aurora flared green across the sky and sent great reflected streamers across the water." The northern lights were so prominent and dramatic that the *Minneapolis Star Tribune* ran an editorial describing the event:

> *On August 22, many* [people] *in the Upper Midwest were lucky, as flaming aurorae fired the sky nearly all night. These were not the colorful ribbon candy sometimes seen near the horizon, nor the charged laundry flapping in the solar breeze, but flashes of illumination shooting up toward a central point overhead like light rays escaping the smoke hole of a cosmic tepee... One, like spectral smoke, the rays of light congealed into a shape—a bird of paradise? a phoenix?—at the center of the heavens. And then it flew away... The northern lights occur at unpredictable intervals, most commonly clustered in the months around the equinoxes, with greater intensity at times of exceptional sunspot activity.*

After the old guys had gone to bed, Eddy, Jonathan and I stretched out on our backs and lay watching the show. As so often happens when people are away from city lights and confronted with the splendor of the night sky, we began talking about cosmic subjects. How old are the stars? How far away are they? For how many years have humans looked up at them? Jonathan was fascinated by the concept of light years and how long it might take the light from a distant star to reach us. It was possible, I said, that we were looking at light from a star that no longer existed.

"Wait," said Jonathan. "How can that be?"

"The light remains visible because of the time it takes to reach us," I said. "When you look at the stars, you look back in time."

"I don't get it."

"Theoretically," I said, "if you had a sufficiently powerful telescope, you could see someone or some creature that had died a million years ago standing on a distant planet and waving at us."

"No way."

"It's true," I said. "And if a person living on a distant planet a million years from now had a powerful enough telescope, that person could see us stretched out here on this rock, moving our arms and pointing in their direction, one million years from this evening. In a way, the image of your body carried by light rays into space lives on long after you're dead and gone."

"Let's wave," Eddy suggested. So we did.

In *Runes of the North*, Sig writes about stargazing with his six-year-old grandson, Derek. When a falling star "streaked across the heavens from east to west" in "a glittering cascade of shattered light," his grandson asked why the star had fallen:

> *I tried to explain but his young mind was not ready for talk of disintegrating matter, oxidation, burning in the stratosphere, and the bombardment of the earth with interstellar dust and meteorites. So I simply said:*
>
> *"Stars fall like the leaves of trees; sometimes they get tired of holding on away up there and just let go, and then they fall."*
>
> *My explanation satisfied him completely. There was nothing more to say.*

Our second day on Frost was windy and hazy. On a day trip to Octopus, we saw an eagle soaring overhead and watched three river otters climb up on the shore and splash back into the water. In the pool by the waterfall, a bass struck my line three times. With Eddy and Jonathan paddling with Bill, I had a chance to paddle with Dad, which I had missed doing both last year and this year.

During the night, I was awakened by an odd sensation. Something had pricked my finger. Or was I dreaming? I sat up and listened, but all I heard was the wind stirring the pines overhead. After a moment, a loon wailed from somewhere far across the lake. Of the four calls that loons make, the wail is my favorite. I lay down, expectant, hopeful. The loon wailed again, hitting two notes. Please, one more, I begged silently. Again, the loon wailed, and this time it hit the third high note, the one I especially love. Surely, that three-note song is one of the most beautiful sounds on the planet. I closed my eyes, hoping it would continue singing, and it did. Each time it hit that third note, I felt content, but in the next moment I found myself longing for more. Would I ever be satisfied? After a while, another loon joined in, and their songs came at intervals, sometimes overlapping. Then I heard another sound. Something had scurried across the tent floor. I reached for my flashlight and fumbled with the switch. Caught in the beam were two beady black eyes peering at me. It was a mouse. I considered ignoring it, but I knew I wouldn't be able to sleep until it was evicted, so I woke the two groggy boys, and the hunt was on.

First, we tried to shoo it out, with no success. There was too much clutter in the tent, too many convenient places for it to hide. Finally, Eddy and Jonathan stood up in their sleeping bags and potato-sacked outside, where they stood hunched, watching the show as I emptied the tent of its contents, one item at a time. Every time I picked something up and tossed it out, the mouse darted into a new refuge. Finally, I got my break when the mouse slipped into one of my running shoes. Grabbing the shoe, I flipped it outside, returning the critter to its natural environment. The boys, still not completely awake, crawled back into the tent and immediately fell asleep while I lay wondering how—and why—it had gotten in. The only thing I could figure out was that it had squeezed through a small gap at the end of the zipper and was looking for food or warmth.

THE NEXT DAY, we paddled and portaged the route from Frost to the north end of Sawbill in a driving rain. Standing in ankle-deep mud at the beginning of one of the portages, I lifted the canoe, and as I hoisted it overhead, two rivulets of cold water ran along the gunwales and down the sleeves of my rain suit. Then, as I started down the trail, a horde of mosquitoes joined me under the shelter of the canoe and began paying visits to the back of my neck. Oh, well, I thought, canoeing isn't all bliss. There are times of total comfort and contentment, and there are times of intense discomfort and misery. It comes with the territory. "We have become too 'comfortized,'" Calvin Rutstrum observes in *Once Upon a Wilderness.* Attitude is everything. Sig had a nice way of making that point in that documentary film:

> *When I was guiding, one of the old-timers told me, he said, "Sig, No matter how wet and cold you are, you're always warm and dry." He said, "Remember that." Well I remembered it for fifty years…If you believe you're going to be cold and miserable, you'll be cold and miserable, but if you just ignore it, learn to live with it, why you can be warm and dry no matter how wet you are.*

Years later, Douglas Wood picked up on the same theme in a story called "The Wildness Within," published in the *Boundary Waters Journal*:

> *I was heading home from a four-day solo canoe trip. I stopped to pull down the brim of my old flop hat against the mizzling rain, then heard a familiar sound. Looking up into a spruce overhead, I saw a chickadee, and another and another…a dozen or so of the little bandits, flitting around the spruce, buzzing, hanging upside down, and generally acting ridiculous…"What ever happens if a chickadee gets depressed? Or doubts himself, or gives up?" I sat there a long time, and I guess I decided that the fact there are so many*

> *chickadees, that they stay all through the winter, and that I was sitting there watching them in the freezing rain, kind of answered my question. They reminded me of the old woodsman's adage, "No matter how cold and wet you are, you're always warm and dry."*

Of course, there's always the other side of the argument. For some people, no matter how warm and dry they were most of the time, what they remember is that they were really cold and wet part of the time. In his weekly "The Old Scout" newspaper column, Garrison Keillor articulates the half-empty rather than half-full take on wilderness canoeing as only Keillor can:

> *What truly cheers me up through these dog days of summer is the thought that two old friends of mine are up north on a canoe trip in the Boundary Waters Canoe Area and that I am not there with them. I am here, reading the paper, and if I wanted to go to a movie, I could go, and if I wished to use a flush toilet, I could do that, too. But for the grace of God, I could be sitting on the ground, filthy, embittered, a homeless person, eating freeze-dried food and listening to the Master Woodsman tell you what a great experience you're having and meanwhile the woods are not lovely, just dark and deep, and a cloud of mosquitoes has come out to avenge the white man's colonizing of North America. I have been on canoe trips, I know what goes on.*

With the boys paddling hard and the wind on our backs, we made good time. Still, it was a long day. Although we tried to imagine ourselves warm and dry, everyone was tired, wet and cold when we reached our campsite in the middle of the afternoon, so we pitched our tents, unrolled our sleeping bags, crawled inside and slept for hours.

That evening, while Bill and Dad fixed dinner, I tried to persuade Eddy and Jonathan to go fishing again, but they weren't interested, so I went for a paddle around the island by myself. This was the second year in a row Eddy hadn't caught a fish. Back on shore, I found a dry rock under a cedar tree, had a seat and carved on Eddy's ball-in-a-box, wondering if I had sat on that same rock on an earlier trip. After a while, I unzipped the tent door as quietly as I could and climbed into my sleeping bag. As I lay listening to the rain pattering on the tent, I thought of Sig's description in *Listening Point*:

> *I like to hear the rain come down on a tent. I am close to it then, as close as one can be without actually being in it. I have slept in many primitive shelters, under overhanging cliffs, in lean-tos made of spruce boughs and birchbark,*

> *in little cabins roofed with poles and sod. I have slept under canoes and boats and under the spreading branches of pines and balsams, but none of these places gives me quite the feeling I get when sleeping in a tent.*

I haven't slept in as many primitive shelters as Sig did, but I know the protected feeling he describes. I love how a tent provides shelter without creating much of a barrier. It protects you from the elements without completely separating you from the natural world. In *Boundary Waters: The Grace of the Wild*, Paul Gruchow writes, "I am not strong, nor well-conditioned, nor physically adept, nor fearless, but I am stubborn and curious and, despite my inadequacies, most of the happiest moments of my life have occurred in nature."

For me, some of the happiest moments in my life have been spent in a tent, deep in the woods, far from civilization, with people I love.

11
Kate at Last

In 1993, Kate came on a canoe trip. At last.

I was delighted to have her with us. I wanted to share my passion for the wilderness with her, as I had done with her mother, and I wanted her to love the Boundary Waters wilderness as much as I did. Like her brother, she was bold and adventurous, and I had no doubt she would feel comfortable exploring the woods and the lakes.

Kate was now twelve years old. We had moved our trip from our traditional third week in August to the first week in August so that Eddy and I could go on a Boy Scout backpacking trip to the Wind River Mountains in Wyoming. As Eddy and I were packing for this trip, my friend Jim called with the disappointing news that he would have to cancel because his mother was ill—he was afraid it might be cancer. I was sorry to hear the news and sorry not to have Jim's company and conversation this year. Then I realized this might be my opportunity to take Kate. When she and Debbie returned from her ice-skating lesson, Eddy asked her if she wanted to go—and she didn't say no.

When Eddy, Jonathan, Kate and I pulled into the Sawbill Canoe Outfitters' parking lot, the first thing Kate said when she saw the outfitters' building was: "I thought it would be bigger."

"I thought the same thing the first time I saw it," Eddy said.

We found Dad and Bill inside. They had flown again this year, and a Sawbill crew member had picked them up from Devil's Track Lake. We had made the trip from Minneapolis by car in just over four and a half hours, and they were surprised to see us so soon.

As Bill Hansen replaced some rivets I had popped out of my canoe the year before, he told me he was a fan of my newspaper column on effective writing. He said he hadn't realized I was the one writing it. He thought the Dr. Stephen Wilbers he knew from my checks was a medical doctor.

"No," I told him, "I have a PhD in English. The doctor in our family is my brother Larry. He's a pathologist."

That night, we stayed at the Sawbill campground, where we had our traditional first night dinner of steak, potatoes and salad, with a little wine (for the adults) to wash it down. Kate offered to make the pudding.

"Don't feel bad if it turns out runny," I said. "We like it that way. We can never get it to set up on these trips, but everything tastes good out here, so don't worry about it."

Undeterred, she read the instructions on the box, poured the contents into the pot, measured the water and mixed it in. Then she carried the pot down to the shore, put it in the shallow water, and placed a small stone on the lid to hold it in place. When it was time for dessert, she retrieved it.

Dad lifted the lid and said, "Well, look at that."

"I don't believe it," Bill said.

Jonathan, Eddy and I gathered around the pot. For the first time on any of our canoe trips, the pudding had set. Kate smiled proudly.

"Wow, Kate," said Eddy. "Way to go."

"How did you do that?" I asked.

"I just mixed it and chilled it," she said. "I'll do the pudding again the next time we have it."

During the night, it started raining, so in the morning we had to break camp and pack wet equipment. As we were driving the sixteen miles from the Sawbill outfitters and campground to Kawishiwi Lake, a huge bull moose ran out onto the road ahead of us. Rather than running off into the woods, it trotted down the road in front of us for a quarter mile. I was excited for Kate to see a moose at the beginning of her first trip.

"It looks funny," she said, and we all agreed that its odd loping gait viewed from the rear was comical.

Kawishiwi looked good to me, beautiful and familiar. There were six of us in three canoes, and Kate would be paddling with me. As we loaded our canoe, she slipped her small backpack under the bow and then helped load the lighter items. She had never loaded a canoe before, but she seemed to know where things went.

It rained most of the day, but despite the gray weather, everyone was in good spirits. When we arrived on Polly, we saw that the island campsite with the bent tree was occupied, but my other favorite campsite on the north point of the peninsula was open, so we took it. As we were unloading the canoes, the clouds broke for a couple hours—just enough time for us to spread our bags and our three tents on the rocks and dry them out. It started drizzling again during dinner, so I skipped my midnight paddle and settled into the tent with Kate. After a while, Eddy and Jonathan joined us, and I read Olive Ann Burns's *Cold Sassy Tree* to the three of them.

Having Kate with me reminded me of her first overnight camping trip. When she was two and a half years old, I had taken her to Baker Park Reserve, a regional park northwest of the Twin Cities. It was a spring trip, cold and wet and windy, but we had a great time, just the two of us. Of course, all that was necessary to meet her expectations was a bag of marshmallows, a Hershey's chocolate bar, some Graham crackers and a tent, so to her it was the perfect outing. The first thing she did after we unloaded the car was trip on the metal fire ring and fall backward into the ashes, but fortunately I hadn't built a fire yet, and she wasn't hurt. I had come directly from a wedding reception, and when I told her I had to change my pants, she asked me if I had gone pee pee.

"No," I told her, "I just want to change into my camping clothes."

After dinner, I spread a blanket under a tree to keep us out of the drizzle, and we sat eating our s'mores and listening to the rain. When she leaned her head on my shoulder, I felt like the happiest man in the world.

After Eddy and Jonathan returned to their tent, Kate opened her neatly packed backpack and took out her pajamas.

"Looks like you did a nice job packing," I said. She had worked from a list I had given her, with assistance from her mother and brother. "What's that?" I said, pointing to what looked like a piece of white paraffin in a clear plastic bag.

"Eddy told me I couldn't bring deodorant because it weighed too much and I wouldn't need it anyway because we would swim every day."

I laughed.

"I told him we weren't going to shower for a week so I was bringing some. Then he said it would be okay to bring some if I took it out of the container. All he brought was one change of clothing and no underpants."

"No underpants?"

"He's wearing his black biker shorts, which he said would stay clean because he would wear them swimming."

Kate and Steve, the summer they first camped together.

Kate with her eye on two boxes of pudding. Steve and Bill cooking dinner to the best of their abilities.

The next day, the weather cleared to a partly cloudy, cool day. Dad, Bill, Kate and I started on a day trip down the Lady Chain, with the boys staying on Polly to paddle around and explore. I was hoping we would make it all the way to Hazel. I wanted Kate to see my favorite Boundary Waters lake and my favorite campsite. I wanted her to explore the rocky stream leading out of the lake and to skip some rocks on the far campsite. I wanted her to experience the wilderness as I had explored Missanabie and Biscotasi Lakes north of Toronto as a Boy Scout and as Eddy had explored the Boundary Waters wilderness on his first trip ten years ago. And then I remembered something I had learned when Kate was born. Parenting one child is never the same as parenting another, even though you love them both and both are precious to you. As with your friends, no two people are alike. They inhabit their own worlds; they have their own ways of taking things in, their own ways of reacting to events. I needed to learn not to compare one child's experience with the other's, not to expect them to be the same. I wanted to be as appreciative of the second child's reactions as I was of the first child's. Kate's presence in the Boundary Waters was a reminder that every day in the wilderness was a new day, that no two days were exactly the same and that if you expected to enjoy one trip in the same way you enjoyed the last one, you risked missing out on the uniqueness of your present experience.

Kate and I pulled alongside Dad and Bill's canoe.

"What do you think?" I asked.

"I don't think we have enough time to make it there and back," Dad said. "Better save Hazel for another trip."

After we turned around, I caught a small northern in a pool by the portage, and Kate seemed to enjoy watching me pull it into the canoe. On the way back to Polly, Dad and Bill attempted to shoot some rapids rather than portage around them. When we met up with them again, I noticed they were wet.

"We capsized," Dad said. "And we lost a life jacket."

"But we found it downstream," Bill said.

Back on Polly, we saw the boys in the bay east of the peninsula where we were camped. They had pulled their canoe over to a small island and were jumping off the rock ledge into the water. When Kate saw what they were doing, she wanted to give it a try.

"Is the water cold?" she asked.

"It's a little chilly," I said, "but you'll be fine."

Despite a chill wind and a cloudy sky, she climbed up to the top of the rock, about twelve feet high. Without a moment's hesitation, she jumped.

Dad and Bill, somewhat damp from having capsized while shooting rapids.

"Wow, that was brave," I said when her head popped above the surface, her eyes open wide.

"Dad, I jump all the time in gymnastics," she said.

I hadn't thought of her routines on the vault, the bars and the beam, but it was true. Not only did she jump into the air, but while she was up there she did somersaults and then had to land on her feet.

Back at camp, we ate dinner and finished off our box of wine, which we refer to as "Chateau Ripple" because Larry had once called it that. Then we talked about how good the pudding was our first night in the campground and watched the sunset from the flat rock. Jonathan, who had enjoyed stargazing so much the year before, was eager to see the northern lights, so we walked to the point, stretched out on the rock and stared up at the night sky for a long time; finally, we did see a hint of them.

"Those are the northern lights," I said to Kate. "The aurora borealis. That's what they look like."

"It looks like a cloud," Kate said.

"Well, sometimes they're brighter," I said.

"And sometimes they turn different colors," Eddy said.

"What kinds of colors?" she asked.

"Red and green," I said.

"And sometimes they look like curtains waving in the sky," Eddy said.

"It just looks like a cloud," Kate said.

"Can you really see back in time when you look at the stars?" Jonathan asked.

His question took the conversation in a familiar direction. We talked about the vastness of the universe and how light from a distant star took a long time to reach us, even when it traveled at the speed of light, and how the light from stars we were seeing that night had actually begun its journey many years earlier.

"That makes sense," Kate said.

"It does?" said Jonathan.

"Sure. Things don't happen all at once," she said.

"I don't know," said Jonathan. "It blows my mind."

"I think it's cool," said Eddy. "Let's wave"

"Why would we wave?" asked Kate.

"So living things on some star trillions of miles away can see us millions of years from now," said Eddy.

"That's silly," Kate said. Nevertheless, she waved.

The next morning, we awoke to a clear, blue sky without a cloud. With the water high this year, we saved some time by skipping the portages leading from Polly and shot some easy rapids. Kate was a strong paddler—steady and uncomplaining—and she did a good job of helping me steer. She was quite the athlete, with good upper-body strength from gymnastics. She seemed undaunted by the challenges of the trip, meeting each one with calm determination. As I knew they would, Bill and Dad have told her several times how pleased they were that she came. I lent Bill a pair of shorts for swimming—the only accommodation we made to being a mixed group.

Although the clouds were building, it was a gorgeous day as we traveled north from Polly to Koma. At the end of the portage to Malberg, I showed Kate the boulder by the mouth of the stream and told her how it had become a kind of marker in my life. As I loaded our gear, I looked back and saw her standing where I had left her, looking at the boulder. Then we paddled the length of the lake and found the campsite on the northwest portage open. When Eddy pointed out the big rock by the tent site and the rock ledge by the "back door," I realized this was the campsite where the bear had swum across the channel and spooked my friend Jim.

It was fun to see Kate interacting with the guys on the trip. She had a delightful laugh when one of the boys did something entertaining. She was willing to give

Kate—still not crazy about bugs—with her fiancé, Markus, in 2006.

fishing a try, although she didn't seem to care if she caught anything or not. As a result of being here the first week rather than the third week in August, we were encountering more people and more insects. The guys were pretty accustomed to the mosquitoes, but I could tell they were pestering Kate, who applied insect repellent and pulled a net over her head at the first sign of a bug.

After we had set up our tent, she unrolled her sleeping bag, and I tucked her in for a nap. "Are you doing all right?" I asked. "Are you having fun?"

"I'm doing fine, Dad," she said as she closed her eyes.

I hoped she was. Even if she didn't end up loving the Boundary Waters wilderness, I wanted her to like it well enough that she would come again. At twelve, her life was already getting busy with school events, sports and social activities, and I hoped the Boundary Waters would be a way for us to spend time together in the years ahead.

As I climbed out of the tent the next morning, Bill greeted me with his customary "Coffee's ready." Love that guy. Kate was tired, but she agreed to take a day trip to Beaver. Eddy told me that because he hadn't caught a fish for his last two trips, he really wanted to catch one this year.

Fortunately, we had a strong tailwind as we traveled north, so we didn't have to paddle hard. While walking the portage to the Kawishiwi River, I passed the familiar slanted rock and the meadow, which was water-filled this year, and both rock and meadow seemed like old friends. As I lowered the canoe at the end of the portage, I heard Kate say, "Oh, look, Dad!" Spreading across the river was a carpet of white water lilies. I knelt beside her, thrilled that she was thrilled. Jaques describes a similar scene on her trip:

> *White water lilies lay on the black water; white birches, delicate poplars, and dark cedars were mingled on three sides. On the fourth was a gigantic hill, with straight Norway pines towering up magnificently between moss-deep rocks. Their strength was a powerful contrast to all the lacelike beauty nearby.*

For Jaques and for us, it wasn't just the beauty that delighted us; it was the surprise of beauty in the midst of such rough terrain.

On Beaver, we rested and lunched on a campsite with a nice jumping rock. Eddy played rough with me in the water. He's getting big and strong. Dad liked the look of the campsite. It was pretty, but I didn't think it was exceptional. Then I noticed that the last campers had left a large pile of split wood stacked near the fire grate. "Make a note of this campsite in your log," Dad said. "It's a beauty." So noted.

THE NEXT DAY, we made an early start. It was warmer than the day before. As we traveled from Malberg to Kawasachong, the boys no longer lagged behind, and they were now portaging their own canoe. We raced, bumped and laughed in the narrows. Still no fish.

Then, on Kawishiwi Lake, it happened. I caught a northern in the north part of the lake, near the reed beds off the east shore. Kate was in the canoe with me. Unlike her mother, she didn't seem disgusted by its massive head and huge mouth. Then I caught another, a big one, easily three pounds. That night, we had our customary fish dinner. Without those two fish, we would have been eating our backup meal of Kraft cheese macaroni dinner and leftovers. We paddled to camp, and I persuaded Eddy and Jonathan to give it a try. We went back out. Eddy had no luck, but Jonathan brought two to the canoe, although he couldn't get them in. After a while, I realized the boys were more interested in watching a group of girls camped at the next site than in fishing. After dinner, the breeze died, and we retreated to the tents to escape the bugs. I was reading to Kate when Eddy asked if he could join us and climbed into the tent. As he settled in next to me, I realized how much I had missed sharing a tent with him this year.

After the mosquitoes had quieted down, Kate and I ventured back outside for marshmallows. I built up the fire and sharpened a stick for her. She held her marshmallow close but not too close to the glowing coals, turning it continuously until it was an even golden brown all around. I chuckled when I thought of the scorched nuggets Eddy typically roasted. I placed two rectangles of Hershey's chocolate on half a graham cracker and then sandwiched her perfectly roasted, soft, gooey marshmallow between that half cracker and its mate. "This is going to be really good," I said.

"Want me to make you one, Daddy?" she asked.

There was only one answer to that question.

Before tucking her into bed for the night, I accompanied her to the biffy, illuminating the throne for her with my flashlight and then standing a discrete distance away. Guys just pee in the woods. For girls, some things about camping were less convenient. Kate, however, seemed unperturbed by the dark path or the night sounds in the brush. In *Northern Waters*, Jan Zita Grover describes how an intimate knowledge of her surroundings helped her overcome some of the obstacles a woman might face in the wilderness:

> *That I can walk these woods in what feels like safety, touch the trees under darkness and know who they are, wade these waters I cannot see, yet know what fish they hold and what small bottom-dwelling creatures they give life to, confers a kind of sympathetic magic on me. I feel strong as these trees, timeless as these waters, sexless, no longer a human woman but a human animal.*

As we walked the narrow path back to the tents, I asked Kate if she felt comfortable in the wilderness at night.

"Yes," she said. "There's less to be afraid of here than in the city."

"Are you afraid in the city?"

"Well, no, not exactly. But I feel safer here."

Our south Minneapolis neighborhood is relatively safe, but as a friend who works for the Bureau of Criminal Apprehension once said to me, statistics don't matter when you're the victim of a crime. I thought again of Grover, who recognizes that being unafraid of the night is "a luxury" unavailable to women of lower economic status:

> *I am able to enjoy this sense of boundlessness, this lack of gender-consciousness, of self-consciousness, because by background I am sufficiently privileged to dare my nights out-of-doors. What, she asks, if I were a woman who had grown up where night sang only of terror in the keys of*

A young girl at ease in the wilderness.

> *rape, muggings, break-ins—would I still view the fall of darkness as a source of pleasure? If I had dwelled only among crummy city streets and learned only streetwise ways, would I see the North Woods with their wild sounds and movements, their cloistering trees and open bogs, as comforting?*

It's a question, I suppose, all women who venture out at night must ask, and it bothered me that my daughter was more likely to ask it than my son.

"I still think you were brave to jump off that high rock," I said. "You should have seen your eyes when you came out of the water. They were as big as saucers."

"That was because the water was freezing," she said. "You told me it wouldn't be that cold, but it felt like a thousand pins were shooting into my skin. It was the coldest water I've even been in."

"I'm sorry, Sweetheart. Was it *that* cold?"

"It was *that* cold."

"Well, I'm still proud of you for jumping."

After tucking her into bed, I went for my midnight paddle. As usual, the wilderness at night didn't disappoint me. The stars were brilliant, lightning flashed on the southern horizon and shooting stars zipped across the sky from the Perseid meteor shower, a product of the Swift-Tuttle comet having passed through the earth's orbit last September, as it does every 130 years, leaving lots of good debris up there to be spectacularly incinerated in our atmosphere. As I paddled back toward camp, an owl hooted. It was a deep, resonant, luxurious sound. "In many cultures the hoot of an owl in the night is heard as the herald of death," Paul Gruchow writes in *Boundary Waters: The Grace of the Wild.* Like Gruchow, I was not alarmed by the prospect of death: "This would be, I thought, a good moment to die if it came to that. It seemed to me as reliable a test of happiness as any: to be in a place where one would be content to die."

I beached my canoe and tucked my paddle and life jacket beneath it. Then I walked silently to the cluster of three tents, which were pitched near one another, and I climbed into ours, where I found Kate sleeping peacefully.

THE NEXT MORNING, our last of the trip, was a beautiful, calm, sunny day. As we paddled across the lake, I watched the muscles in Kate's arms and back move in rhythm to her smooth, powerful stroke.

"You're quite a canoeist," I said. "Did you like the Boundary Waters?"

At first she didn't respond. Then she said, "It was fun, but I missed doing a lot of things at home."

Cindy and Bill Hansen, two of the nicest people to ever run a canoe-outfitting business.

Well, it wasn't a rave review, but she had come, and she did seem to have enjoyed herself. She had handled herself with a calm, quiet confidence, and she had impressed everyone with how able she was in the canoe and around the campsite.

Back at the outfitters, Cindy said we were fortunate to have had the best weather they had all year. We dropped Dad and Bill at the new Grand Marais airport, which had been carved into the woods up the hill from the old Devil's Track airport, farther from the big lake and its wind shears. As he said goodbye, Dad gave each of us a long hug.

12

A Meltdown and a Broken Bow

Other than leaving my fishing pole and our frozen steaks on the porch at home, we made a good start this year, 1994. With his learner's permit, Eddy helped out with the driving. Eddy's friend Jonathan was with us again this year, but Kate decided not to come. In her place was Bill's son, Paul. So this year, Dad and I paddled together. It was good to be in a canoe with him again.

When we arrived at Sawbill, Cindy laughed when she heard me call Debbie and tell her I had left our steaks for her. Then Cindy picked some out for us from their supply.

As we relaxed on our Cherokee Mouse Island Campsite, everyone was tired, but good tired. After setting up camp, Dad and Eddy paddled over to the little island and jumped off the jumping rock while I paddled around the larger island fishing. Although no fish were tempted by what I was offering, I enjoyed drifting through the mustard green light cast by the sunlit cedars along the shore. No other tress cast that special light on the water. Only cedars do.

As I rounded the point of the island, I thought about our cabin search. Debbie and I had begun looking for lake property. In the process, we had become preoccupied with the features that make lake property desirable: driving time from home, size and type of lake, water quality, lake bottom (sand or muck), tree cover, orientation of the cabin on the lake (north, south, east or west facing), style and condition of the cabin, distance from other cabins, relative privacy, places to walk, proximity to ski trails and distance to interesting towns and places to buy groceries. Now that I was back in the Boundary Waters wilderness, I was reminded that what I was seeing and experiencing here could not be measured, priced or owned. The Boundary Waters was not a piece of property. It was a precious resource, a relatively undisturbed remnant of the natural world. To own a part of it would diminish its value and significance. Developing it would alter its character, and withdrawing it from the public domain would remove it from our national heritage.

Our second day on Cherokee was partly cloudy with a couple of brief showers, but the sun came out at the right times. On a day trip to Town Lake, Eddy and Jonathan carried the canoe between them, with one person on either side. We were proud of them, even though they let it drift away after they put it into the water. Bill and Paul retrieved it, and we all had a good laugh.

"That will have to go in the log," Dad said. Sorry, boys, but there it is.

With its steep shoreline and clear water, Town is a gem. We warmed ourselves in the sun on our lunch rock and then waded into the water for a swim, taking care not to slip on the slippery rocks. Later, Dad had a northern on his line but lost it when it dove. Then he hooked a five-pound beauty. I missed it twice with the net before we finally brought it in.

Our fish dinner that night was terrific, as it always was, with everyone having seconds. The secret, which I learned from Bill, was to fry the fish over a very hot fire so that the batter got a toasted taste. After we had eaten our fill, I took Eddy over to the thirty-foot jumping rock on the main shore, a significantly higher cliff than the one on the small island. He was determined to "get it done" this year, he said, and we did. He was fearless, and I was impressed. As anyone who has ever jumped off a cliff knows, it looks much higher when you're on top looking down than it does when you're at water level looking up.

From Cherokee, we traveled to South Temperance, a familiar route. From time to time, I glanced at my watch (a Spalding sports watch Eddy had given me). In past years, I've gone without one, preferring to go by natural time, but people always talked about what time it was anyway so I gave in and decided to stop being the purist. I had to admit, it was helpful to know when it was time to start looking for a campsite or to start cooking dinner.

Before turning in, I stood at the tip of the granite rock shoreline, gazing at the moon and listening to the echoing wails of the loons. At every turn on this trip, I was encountering memories from past trips. This was the campsite where Dad had talked about retirement in 1985. We had stayed here again in 1990. The portage on the far side of the lake was where Eddy had lost his Swiss Army knife on his second trip. Two years ago, Eddy and Jonathan had walked along the sand beach on Frost Lake when Jonathan was more than a foot taller and easily thirty pounds heavier than Eddy. This year, they were about the same height, and they were double-packing on the portages—that is, they carried one pack on their backs and a second one on front—and they carried the canoe just like the older guys. I realized how changes in adult bodies from one year to the next were hardly noticeable, but in children and adolescents the changes were remarkable.

After dinner, I sat with Paul on the west-facing rocks a little way from the campsite, carving on the cedar ball-in-a-box I was making for Eddy. The little ball inside the four pillars was nearly round now. One of these years I would finish it, but I was in no hurry. It wouldn't bother me to spend a lifetime working on it.

THE NEXT DAY, we took a day trip to Brule. I looked for the impression in the rocks left by Sam's butt in 1990 when he was soaking his sunburned and swollen legs in the cold water, but we couldn't find it. I caught a northern and a smallmouth and had another bronzeback on my line, but it jumped and spit out my lure. I love how they do that. Then we climbed the pink granite boulder field and took in the spectacular view of Brule and the nearby lake. We explored what looked like a little-used mountain trail, but it turned out to be the portage to Wench. Back at camp, everyone rested and bathed with warm water from the pots Dad had left in the sun on the fire grate. It was a typical camp scene for us: me with my log, Dad with Louis L'Amour, Bill and Paul with their cards and cribbage board and Jonathan and Eddy on an expedition to find a lookout with a good view of the lake. When the boys returned, I talked Eddy into going fishing. I wanted to see if he could break his string of trips with no fish.

As we gathered our gear, Dad said, "You look like two men with a mission."

"We're not coming back until Eddy catches a fish," I declared.

We paddled out to a rock point about fifteen feet from shore and cast our lines. After getting a couple of strikes, Eddy hooked one, a small northern, and pulled it in. Life can be so sweet.

The next day was a travel day to Burnt—gorgeous, mostly sunny, a few scattered clouds, very light breeze. Yesterday's haze had dissipated overnight, so the sun was its normal yellowish color rather than reddish white, and the sky was azure blue. Packing and breaking camp went well, and we were off the campsite by seven thirty.

With Eddy and Jonathan carrying full loads, we were able to single-portage the five portages to Burnt, making it there before noon. The paddle down the Temperance River was beautiful, as it always is. I hadn't remembered the wild rice being so plentiful or how the amber stalks leaned in unison with the current. On the fifty-four-rod portage, Dad startled a bull moose, which took a good look at him and then crashed down the portage path. When Jonathan and I went back to signal the others that the campsite on Smoke was open, we saw a cow moose and calf swimming not far from the portage. Bill and I wanted to go on to Flame, but Dad seemed hesitant, so we went back to the campsite across from the portage and ate lunch. Eddy was exhausted and hungry. He snapped at Jonathan and then turned to me.

"All you do is keep pushing and pushing it," he said, almost shouting.

I felt awful. As trip leader, I should have suggested more breaks along the way or an earlier lunch.

Eddy is sitting with me by the fire now, not talking, intent on making a bow—carving it, soaking it and heating it over the fire. Earlier, he asked me for some cord. As he was stringing the bent stick, it broke. "I knew that would happen," he said. "I should have soaked it longer." Apparently unperturbed, he recarved the broken end, making it a shorter bow.

After dinner, we retired to the west-facing rock to watch the sunset. I couldn't help but think about how nice it would be to find a cabin facing west. As we sat there watching the light fade from the sky, I carved on Eddy's cedar ball-in-a box, straightening the two ends a bit. Dad, Bill and Paul can't believe how long it's taking me to finish it, but I'm enjoying the process. The only time I carve on it is in the Boundary Waters wilderness, and then only when I'm in the mood. Eddy looked at it and said it looked "crude." Then, without looking at me, he said, "But it looks better now that you've squared up the columns."

"After five minutes of doing what you're doing," Paul said, "I would have to go hit something."

Both Dad and Eddy declined my invitation for an evening paddle. Then, as I was pushing off from shore, Eddy said, "Hey, wait for me." We paddled out just as the blue was fading from the sky and the moon was rising over the trees behind our campsite. Silhouetted by the western light was the black outline of a loon, its body motionless and graceful as it propelled itself across the lake. We didn't talk much, but I was glad Eddy had come out on the lake with me—and back at the campfire, I was glad to have him sit near me. He held his bow, examining it and turning it over in his hand.

"It doesn't work well," he said, "but it was good practice."

I wondered if he would come next year. As it turned out, he wouldn't come again for seven years.

13

No Youngsters and One Moose

Eddy, Kate, Jonathan and Paul couldn't make it this year, 1995, so it was just Dad, Bill and me. Kate thought about coming but decided not to. Eddy stayed home to play football. His mother and I have encouraged him to try new things, to be open to new experiences, and he has. He told us he had always wanted to play; he wished we had let him, and this year he was going to. So he stayed home to train with the Washburn High School team. The coaches love having him on the team because he takes school seriously, does his homework and sets a good example for the other football players. I understood Kate's decision, and I was pleased Eddy was doing something he had always wanted to do, but I missed having them on the trip.

I didn't write in my log this year. I started keeping it in the early 1980s after my first few canoe trips with Dad. In addition to the entries, I've entered the chronology of years, names and lakes on the inside covers. But this year, whenever I found myself with time to write—when I was leaning against a rock by the lake in the morning sun, sitting in the cool night air by the campfire or stretched out warm and dry in my sleeping bag with the rain beating its soothing rhythm above my head—I wasn't in the mood. I also didn't carve on Eddy's ball-in-a-box.

Our first night out, we stayed on the west-facing campsite by the island on the peninsula on Polly. As Bill was cooking our steak and potato dinner, I offered to make the pudding, which turned out runny. I pulled out the stack of blue plastic cups from the cook kit pack. They were marked D, B, S, E and K. Every few years, we had to retrace the letters, which would wear off with

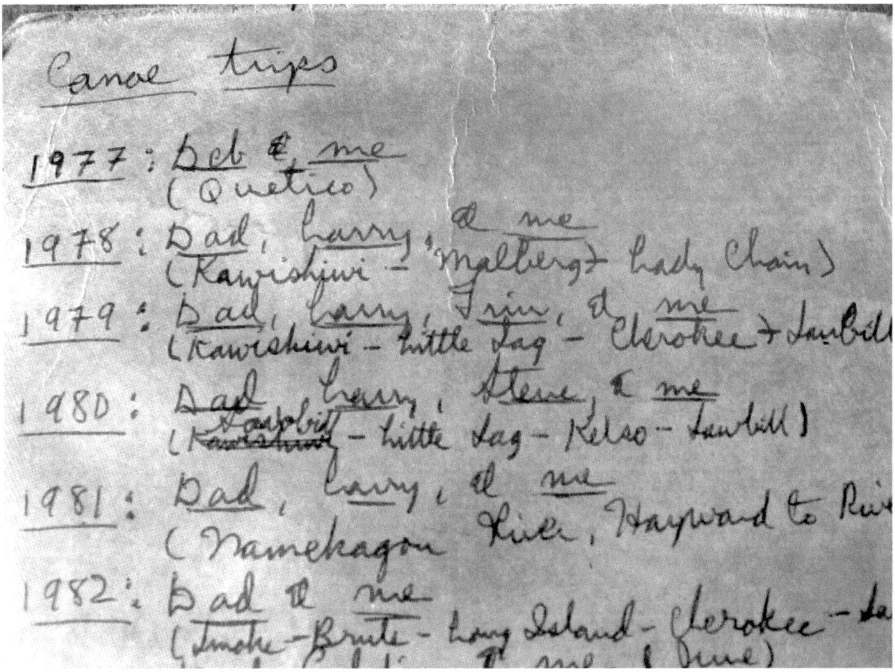

Canoe trips

1977: Deb & me
(Quetico)
1978: Dad, Larry, & me
(Kawishiwi - Malberg - Lady Chain)
1979: Dad, Larry, Jim, & me
(Kawishiwi - Little Sag - Cherokee + Sawbill
1980: Dad, Larry, Steve, & me
(Sawbill - Little Sag - Kelso - Sawbill)
1981: Dad, Larry, & me
(Namekagon River, Hayward to
1982: Dad & me
(Smoke - Brule - Long Island - Cherokee -

A log of wilderness canoe trips taken, dating from 1977.

use, but it was a good system for not having to continually ask whose cup was whose. I placed the cups marked D, B and S on a flat rock near the fire and returned the cups marked E and K to the pack.

On our day trip to Hazel, we stopped for lunch on Rock Skipping Campsite. It had been four years since we had been on Hazel and visited this campsite. The fallen jack pine on the far campsite lay nearly flat on the smooth rock. I wondered which would come first, the steady dismemberment by campers in search of firewood or the gradual process of rot and decay. Then the three of us climbed back into our canoe, paddled to the portage on the west end of the lake and headed down the Phoebe River. On the way back to Polly, we saw a moose feeding in the shallows.

14

One Foursome and One Lost Girl

For the next few years, we took a run of trips with just the four of us: Dad, Bill, his son Paul and me. We became an efficient team that knew one another's habits and preferred chores. Dad organized the cook kit, did the dishes and looped the rope over a tree branch to hang the food pack. Bill gathered, sawed and split wood, did most of the cooking, started the morning fires and made the morning coffee. Paul and I switched from one task to another as needed, and as the years went by, we became the bearers of the canoes over portages, although the old guys continued to haul plenty of weight, with Dad double-packing and Bill often reaching for the food pack before anyone else could grab it. The only thing that seemed a bit unfair was that the burden of bringing in fish for dinner generally fell to me, but I never complained.

And always, there was the beauty of the Boundary Waters wilderness. There was the silence, the solitude and the dignity of the natural order. There were times when the lakes and rocks and trees were merely a backdrop for the drama of our expeditions, and there were moments of intense awareness when I felt myself intimately and inextricably linked to my environment. For me, these times most often occurred alone in a canoe at night. For Sig, these moments of "attunement," as he called them, occurred early in the morning, just before daybreak. He describes one such moment, when "the cosmos could be felt," in *The Singing Wilderness*:

> *It was before dawn, that period of hush before the birds had begun to sing. The lake was breathing softly as in sleep; rising and falling, it seemed to me to absorb like a great sponge all the sounds of the earth. It was a time of quiet—no wind rustling the leaves, no lapping of the water, no*

> *calling of animals or birds. But I listened just the same, straining with all my faculties toward something—I knew not what—trying to catch the meanings that were there in that moment before the lifting of the dark.*

It was then, "standing there alone," that Sig "felt alive, more aware and receptive than ever before: A shout or a movement would have destroyed the spell. This was a time for silence, for being in pace with ancient rhythms and timelessness, the breathing of the lake, the slow growth of living things."

IN 1997, WE PUT IN on Kawishiwi Lake and headed to Kawasachong and from there to Polly. As we paddled the Phoebe River, we passed tall sedges and bogs and then walked the series of short portages to Hazel, where we saw, to our dismay, that the south shore campsite, my favorite, was taken. We paddled over to Rock Skipping Campsite and ate lunch there. The old jack pine was now a half-rotted log lying on the rock shore, completely shorn of its branches. As we were eating, two canoes pulled away from the south shore campsite, so we jumped into our canoes, paddled over and set up camp.

While Bill, Dad and Paul busied themselves with preparing dinner, I picked up the saw and started down the path into the woods to get some more wood. I paused near Eddy's lookout tree. Numbers are only numbers, but they do tell a story. The first time Eddy climbed that tree, it was about sixteen feet tall. Now it was well over forty. The first time I canoed the Boundary Waters wilderness with my father, he was fifty-three and I was twenty-nine. Now he was seventy-two and I was forty-eight. How many more years were left for us? How many for Debbie, Eddy and Kate? How many for all of us?

One week after our trip, which had been cloudy, windy and cold, with the temperature dropping into the forties, a thirteen-year-old girl wandered away from her campsite on Koma, not far from where we had camped. Before she was rescued, she nearly died of exposure.

As reported in the August 31, 1997 *Minneapolis Star Tribune*, Sandy Christiansen was with a group from Bethany Lutheran Church in Minneapolis. Thinking she was camped on an island rather than a peninsula, she went for a walk after dinner. She followed a path into the woods until it disappeared, and she became disoriented. Then it started raining. The temperature dropped to fifty degrees, and not knowing what else to do, she kept walking—for seven hours. She wandered north away from her campsite and was nearing exhaustion when she had a stroke of extraordinarily good luck. She spotted something white on the shoreline she had been following. The white object turned out to be a canoe.

According to the newspaper account, Larry Jedlicka was sleeping alone in his tent on Malberg when he was awakened by an unusual sound. Because it was "so soft and repetitive," he said he thought it might be a wounded bear. Then he recognized the sound as a voice saying, "Help, help."

Jedlicka, a neurologist from New London, Minnesota, had paddled the Boundary Waters wilderness for thirty years. He scrambled out of his tent and "found a girl, soaking wet and shivering, lying on the ground, and softly crying for help."

"She was approaching hypothermia," he said. "If this child hadn't seen that canoe, she probably would have died."

He was the only person camping on that side of the lake. In every other direction, there was no one. He got the girl into some of his dry clothing, and because he knew the members of her church group would be distraught over her disappearance, he decided not to wait until morning but to look for them right away. He packed up his gear and loaded his canoe, and they set out in the darkness.

Malberg is a hub lake, but apparently Sandy was able to describe the location of her campsite in enough detail that Jedlicka knew to head south rather than northwest or northeast. When he found her group, they said they had searched for her until dark. When they couldn't find her, they had decided to wait until daybreak and then paddle back to the Sawbill Trail to get help. Jedlicka didn't fault them for their decision.

"They were five hours from the Sawbill Trail, where they came in," he said. "It was raining and it was night. You just don't take a five-hour trip at night in the Boundary Waters."

Fortunately, Sandy hadn't died. But what if she had wandered west rather than north? What if Jedlicka's canoe had been green or red rather than white? What if he hadn't been so experienced? Unlike the six-year-old boy who had disappeared into the rapids, Sandy was lucky.

The next year, 1998, we spent our last day and night on Flame. After we pitched our tents and gathered wood, I pulled Eddy's ball-in-a-box from my pack. The ball was nearly round, although it still had four creases from where I had freed it from the columns. The trick now was to smooth out those creases without making the ball too small. In the late afternoon, I paddled over to the cliff with the jumping rock and sat there looking out across the lake, alone with my thoughts. Back at camp, a line of dark clouds appeared over the horizon, and Dad, Bill, Paul and I watched a squall hit the far shore and then advance toward us across the lake like a curtain drawn across the water.

15

Eddy's Return, a Moose Bawling in the Woods and a Plethora of Smallies

The year is 2001. I'm on my favorite campsite on my favorite lake in the Boundary Waters wilderness. I'm sitting in the nook by the jack pine that leans over the lake, the one Larry once leaned against and my dad declared the best seat in the house. Earlier today, we paddled over to the far campsite, saw the remains of the old tree and skipped a few stones across the water. I marveled at how Dad could make them fly. One day, I know, I'll return to the Boundary Waters wilderness without him. The years will seem like minutes, and I'll turn around expecting to see him walking the campsite to find a suitable branch to hang the food pack or arranging a pot of soapy water and dirty dishes on a big rock to do cleanup. On the way back to our campsite, we caught a few walleyes and walked the rapids, and later I stood beneath Eddy's lookout tree—all the things I love to do on Hazel.

A few minutes ago, I was carving on Eddy's ball-in-a box. With each knife cut, I exposed bright red where the wood had dulled over time, and each stroke released the sweet aroma of cedar. I held the carving to my nose, and as I inhaled, memories of past canoe trips washed over me. I thought of the easy times—mornings so fresh and sweet I couldn't believe how lucky I was to be alive, an ever-widening region of lakes and forests that delighted us with their unfolding mystery and beauty, long gentle evenings after a hard day's paddle when the air held us in its warm embrace and the sun lingered for hours in the western sky before finally dropping below the pines, brilliant starlit nights when there was magic in the air. And I thought of the hard times—cold, rainy days and nights with wet tents and sleeping bags, fierce headwinds and white-capped waves crashing over the bows of our canoes, lakes with no available campsites and no guarantee of an available campsite on the next lake or the one after that and hordes of mosquitoes that attacked us on portages when our hands were full and descended in swarms at dusk when we wanted to linger by the fire. But they were all good times. Even the bad times were good.

Today is warm, the breeze fresh and invigorating. Above me, the pines are playing their gentle symphony. I love the trees. Like the loons and the granite outcroppings, they are a part of what defines the Boundary Waters wilderness, what gives it its character. "Without the trees, I wouldn't have the same feeling toward the earth as I do now," Sig said in that documentary film. "The trees have become part of me." I'm getting better at identifying the different kinds. Most of what I know about forest ecology I've learned from Bud Heinselman, who describes the trees found in this region as only a scientist could:

> *All of the principal tree species of the central Canadian boreal forest are abundant in the Boundary Waters (black and white spruce, jack pine, balsam fir, tamarack, northern white cedar, quaking aspen, paper birch, and balsam poplar), and they often form extensive forests lacking a significant component of white or red pine. There are also many areas within the virgin forest where white and red pine are abundant, and even some where red maple, red oak, and black ash are common, all typical species of the Great Lakes forests. Yellow birch, basswood, red oak, northern pin oak, bur oak, large-toothed aspen, and red maple also occur, and they all reach their northern limits within or just north of Quetico.*

Realizing any year could be his grandpa's last trip, Eddy decided to join us this year. I'm thrilled to have him back with us. I'm so happy I feel giddy, and I have to restrain myself from talking too much. Eddy last canoed with us when he was fifteen. Now he's twenty-two. Last spring, he graduated from the University of Denver. With his job search, he wasn't able to spend the entire week with us, so he, along with his friend Jonathan, will be with us for only the first part of our trip.

We put in on Sawbill this year. When we were paddling the Phoebe River on the way to the southern campsite on Phoebe Lake, Paul and Bill went ahead of the other two canoes and came upon a moose standing in the water up to its neck. So our search for a whole, live moose had already been successful, at least by part of our crew. Later in the day, we heard a strange sound, which we took to be a moose bawling. We thought it might have been a cow moose calling its calf. Maybe it was an injured animal. That evening during Happy Hour, we talked about politics and our differing views of America, as we often do. It's not a part of a trip I enjoy, but I was proud of the way Jonathan suggested in his gentle way that it's important to ask *why* certain people commit more crimes than others and to understand the underlying causes. Jonathan's mother is Swedish American, his father African American.

It was Eddy who caught our fish dinner. Then, after we had eaten, as the light dimmed from the western sky, I sat with him on the shore of Hazel Lake, and we talked about his job search, the importance of finding meaningful work and our family. Eddy said the scrapbook Kate had made of their trip to Japan was one of the nicest gifts anyone had ever given him.

We were relaxing on our north-facing campsite on the south arm of Grace. It was the third day of our trip. I was sitting beneath a big red pine, working on Eddy's ball-in-a-box. The little ball was now completely round. I took one last stroke with my knife and then turned it over in my hand.

"Here you go," I said, handing it to Eddy.

"Looks pretty good," Dad said.

"Did the ball fall out?" Paul asked.

Bill laughed his deep chuckle.

Eddy tilted it and rolled the ball back and forth inside its four-poster cage. "Thanks, Pop," he said. "You did a nice job."

I had enjoyed the process of carving it, working slowly and deliberately, taking my time, carving on it only when I was in the Boundary Waters wilderness and only when I was in the mood. Carving it was like paddling a canoe. You want to get to where you're going, and you know eventually you will, but there's no point in rushing. The journey itself is as important as the destination.

The next morning after breakfast, Eddy and Jonathan packed up. I helped them load their canoe and then stood on the shore and watched them paddle away. It seemed odd saying goodbye to my son in the Boundary Waters wilderness, watching the slow progress of his canoe as it made its way across the lake, not knowing exactly when I would see him again. I suppose what I was experiencing was a common occurrence for the fur-trading voyageurs in this region, as it was for the pioneers on the prairie. There are no guarantees, not in the wilderness, not on the prairie and not in life. I hoped Eddy would

From left: Paul, Jonathan, Bill, Steve, Larry and Eddy in front of the Sawbill Canoe Outfitters' old store.

Eddy's cedar ball-in-a-box, atop a Sawbill log.

be all right on his own. I hoped he would find his way, and I looked forward to the next time I would see him.

Paddling the Phoebe River to Hazel, we were treated to a profusion of white water lilies, a sight that reminded me of the time Kate and I had marveled at their beauty. Then I thought of the small island in the east bay of Polly. Kate was twelve years old when she jumped from that rock. Now she was twenty. Eight years was a long time in a young girl's life—now a young woman's life. Last year, she completed her sophomore year at Bradley University in Peoria, Illinois. This year, she was transferring to the University of Minnesota. Maybe one day she would canoe with me again.

The fire crackles softly. Everyone except me has gone to bed. I open my log and read a few entries. It's nice to have this record of our trips, but why, I ask myself, have I gone to so much trouble writing it? Why not just enjoy the experience and let the memories take care of themselves? I think of my running friend Steve, who has kept a journal for years, and I remember his telling me he rarely goes back and reads what he has written. For him, the value is in the writing, which causes him to reflect on his day-to-day experiences. Then I think of Bud Heinselman, who describes something about this region, a certain quality, that motivated him to spend his life "studying the forests and bogs of the Boundary Waters and to write this book," *The Boundary Waters Wilderness Ecosystem.* Perhaps this quality, he speculates, is "what motivates many others who have studied or written about wilderness or painted or photographed its moods and scenes." Maybe that was the case for me. "Some of us can never get enough of nature," Heinselman writes. "We do what we do because we love wild places and the mystery that will always exist in lakes, forests, deserts, mountains, and oceans."

Keeping this log has allowed me to relive my wilderness experiences, many of which would otherwise be forgotten and lost. It has allowed me to recall my excitement on first encountering the border lakes region with my wife, to spend some time with my dad when he was younger than I am now, to remember the challenges and joys of taking my four-year-old son on his first trip, to savor the details of my twelve-year-old daughter's introduction to a place I have come to cherish and—perhaps most important—to leave a record of these times for people I love.

Meanwhile, I hope to keep canoeing. If I go as long as my dad has, I have another twenty-five years of canoeing in me. And if I go longer, I have even more.

Canoeing the Boundary Waters wilderness: another twenty-five years?

"Even at the tender age of eighty," Sig said in that film, "my greatest happiness is sitting down and working on this next book." Maybe that will be me one day.

Sig talked about looking for "a spot of blue" at the end of a portage, that glimpse of blue water through the trees that means you've almost arrived, and with shoulders and legs aching, you know that in a few more steps you can put down your equipment, take a little rest and begin the next stage of your journey. "Everyone is looking for a spot of blue," he said in that film. "Without that spot of blue, you don't know where to go. You have no direction in your life."

Maybe someday I'll find my spot of blue. Meanwhile, I'll just keep looking. Who knows what I'll find and where I'll find it?

EPILOGUE

Debbie continues to love the Boundary Waters wilderness from a distance, and she loves that I enjoy going there. In 2002, she made an exception to her "I only sleep in beds" policy when she canoed Michigan's Sylvania Wilderness with our good friends Tom and Babs Zehren. Although we now own a cabin on a Wisconsin lake with good fishing, she has not touched a fishing pole since 1977.

Since that first trip with Debbie in 1977, I've canoed with both of my brothers, Larry and Tim, and with one of my two sisters, Linda, as well as with Linda and Bob's children, Meg and Ted. Although I've not yet canoed with my other sister, Lisa, I *have* canoed with her husband, Bill, and with their son Andrew, as well as with some good friends and neighbors, including two of their daughters and one of their nephews. I've canoed one time with Bill Hansen, in 2001, and I'm hoping we'll go again. If he can get away from work, I'd be happy to provide the gear and equipment, including the sixty-eight-pound lightweight Alumacraft canoe I bought from him in 1987 for $240.

I've taken twenty-two canoe Boundary Waters wilderness trips with my men's group, and we're not done yet. In early September 2011, while camped on an island on Meeds, we debated whether we were seeing a billowing cloud on the horizon or a pyrocumulus cloud from the Pagami Creek fire, which was forty miles away and directly upwind from us. The next day, the fire picked up and ran twenty-five miles straight at us. When it got within fifteen miles, white ash began falling on our campsite, the wind gusted and the lake erupted in whitecaps. Had we known how close it was to us, we

Dad getting his accustomed greeting from Cindy.

Cindy and Bill taking time to help Dad celebrate nearly thirty years of canoeing with Sawbill Canoe Outfitters (August 3, 2010).

might have made a run for it, although leaving the water for a portage trail with an approaching forest fire can be dangerous. The following day, as we were taking out from Poplar, two rangers posted a notice that the entry point was closed.

Dad took his last canoe trip with me in 2007, six years after the present story ends. In the summer of 2010, he and his wife Joan, along with Debbie and me, drove up the North Shore and down the Sawbill Trail so that Dad could see the Hansen family, the Sawbill Canoe Outfitters building and the Sawbill canoe landing one last time. Sadly, Bill Hansen's eighty-nine-year-old father, Frank, died early in the morning on the day of our visit. Nevertheless, Bill drove in from Grand Marais so that he and Cindy could spend some time with us.

In July 2011, I visited Dad in Cincinnati and gave him copies of my newly published book, *A Boundary Waters History: Canoeing Across Time*, which is a brief history of the region and the story of our canoeing together (with an introduction by Bill Hansen). It was a moment I'll never forget. Although Dad had taken his last trip only four years earlier, he was having trouble walking because of a Parkinson's-like illness. I can't wait to give him copies of this book when I see him later this year.

Dad's friend Bill was an eager companion on twenty-two annual trips. He likes to call Dad "the old fart" because Dad is two years older than he. Enthralled by the beauty of the Boundary Waters and unfazed by the hardships of wilderness canoeing, he took his last trip in 2009, when he was eighty-three. His son Paul has canoed with me only thirteen times. Now that Paul is retired, he has no excuse not to add to that number. I hope he does.

Eddy canoed with his grandpa for the last time in 2006. Dad and I began that trip wearing T-shirts with a photo from our 1985 trip. I had had the image printed on the shirts and had given one to Dad. In the photo, Eddy, who was six at the time, is standing between us. He's wearing an orange life jacket and holding the sawed-off paddle his grandpa had fashioned for him. As we were putting in on Kawishiwi Lake twenty-one years later, I suggested we re-create the scene. To approximate the pose, I put an old orange life jacket around my twenty-seven-year-old son's neck. He gave me a look of long-suffering forbearance but didn't protest. After the trip, Dad sent both photos to Bill Hansen, who posted them on the Sawbill website, noting the "dorky" life jacket Eddy was wearing.

On that same trip, as we were paddling to Hazel in the early morning sun, Eddy flipped out of the one-person Prism we had rented from Bill. One moment he was in the canoe; the next he was in the water. His canoe lurched,

Bill and Paul, another father-son combo, in 2009.

Three generations about to embark on a wilderness canoe trip in 1985.

Above: A re-creation of that 1985 venture, twenty-one years later.

Left, fom left: Young father (fifty-six) and elderly son (twenty-seven) with the catch of the day in 2006.

nearly capsized and then righted itself as his head popped out of the water. We paddled over and helped him get the canoe over to a nearby rock.

"I lost my balance," he said, climbing on up the rock, taking off his shirt and climbing back into the canoe. "I knew I was going in, so I just flipped over the side so I wouldn't dump the equipment."

A few days later on Grace, Eddy went fishing after dinner while the old guys (that would include me) played cribbage on the flat rock by the water. He caught ten smallmouths, the most fish he had ever caught in his life, one right after another, in the same reedy bay near the portage to Beth where I had caught

Left: Eddy and cousin Meg in 2010, at the end of the Sawbill-to-Smoke portage.

Below: Eddy and Meg about to enter Flame Lake the fun way, at summer's end.

a bunch five years earlier. Now an accomplished fire spinner and volunteer tai chi instructor, Eddy works as an aide in the psych ward of the University of Minnesota Medical Center, Fairview, and is pursuing a master's in psychology and counseling services at St. Mary's University of Minnesota.

In 2010 and 2011, Eddy canoed with me again, along with his cousin, my niece Meg, who first canoed with me in the Boundary Waters wilderness when she was thirteen. On the first of those two trips, the three of us stayed on Flame Lake and jumped off the rock cliff there about a hundred times and took as many pictures. To say Meg likes the Boundary Waters would be an understatement.

The stronger (and better-looking) crew members: Kate, Debbie and Meg in our south Minneapolis backyard.

For the past two summers, she has worked as a crew member for Sawbill Canoe Outfitters, and she plans to return in the summer of 2012. Both Eddy and Meg are planning to canoe with me again this summer.

Kate, perhaps under the influence of her outdoor-loving husband, Markus, canoed with me again in 2006 and then again in 2007 for Dad's last trip, which I write about in *A Boundary Waters History*. She and Markus came again in 2009 and 2010. Leaving behind her life as a ballroom dance instructor (at least for now), she moved to Colorado soon after our 2010 trip. When I asked her recently about her memories of her first trip, she referred to paddling as "a necessary part of a canoe trip," and she said she loved the beauty and the solitude of the Boundary Waters. She also told me that, as we paddled past Eddy and Jonathan on Polly, Eddy mooned us. This spring, Kate will graduate from the University of Denver with a master's in elementary education, and she will complete her first year of teaching kindergarten. Depending on their job situations, she and Markus will canoe with us this summer. Whether they will be able to get away in the years ahead is an open question, but I am forever hopeful.

REFERENCES AND SOURCES FOR QUOTATIONS

Breining, Greg, and Jerry Stebbins. *Boundary Waters.* Minneapolis, MN: Nodin Press, 1983.

Christensen, Ray, and Steve Kahlenbeck. *The Wilderness World of Sigurd F. Olson.* Documentary film. (Originally produced in 1980 by Filmedia, which later changed its name to ChartHouse; now distributed by Listening Point Foundation, Inc., listeningpointfoundation.org.)

Crowley, Kate, and Mike Link. *Boundary Waters Canoe Area Wilderness.* Stillwater, MN: Voyageur Press, 1987.

———. *Love of Loons.* Stillwater, MN: Voyageur Press, 1988.

Furtman, Michael. *Magic on the Rocks: Canoe Country Pictographs.* Duluth, MN: Birch Portage Press; distributed by Adventure Publications, 2000.

Grover, Jan Zita. *Northern Waters.* Minneapolis, MN: Graywolf Press, 1999.

Gruchow, Paul. *Boundary Waters: The Grace of the Wild.* Minneapolis, MN: Milkweed Editions; distributed by Publishers Group West, 1997.

Hansen, Bill. Annotated map describing canoe routes in the Sawbill Lake area, with commentary about the history of the area and suggestions about things to look for. N.d.

Heinselman, Miron (Bud). *The Boundary Waters Wilderness Ecosystem.* Minneapolis, MN: University of Minnesota Press, 1996.

Jaques, Florence Page: *Canoe Country.* Minneapolis: University of Minnesota Press, 1938. Reprint, 1999.

Keillor, Garrison. "The Master Woodsman Takes a Hike." *Minneapolis Star Tribune*, August 14, 2007.

Klein, Tom. *In Loon Magic*. Ashland, WI: Paper Birch Press, 1985.

Magie, Bill. *A Wonderful Country: The Quetico-Superior Stories of Bill Magie.* Edited by Dave Olesen. N.p.: Sig Olson Environmental Institute, 1984. Reprint, Ely, MN: Raven Productions, 2005.

Manfred, Freya. *Frederick Manfred: A Daughter Remembers*. St. Paul: Minnesota Historical Society Press, 1999.

McPhee, John. *Basin and Range*. New York: Farrar, Straus & Giroux, 1982.

Oberholtzer, Ernest (Ober). "The Ancient Game of Grab: How the Resources of the Ontario-Minnesota Border Lakes are Vanishing into Thin Air." October 1929. Reprint, *The Lakes of Verendrye: A University of the Wilderness*. N.p.: Quetico-Superior Council, n.d.

Olson, Sigurd. *Listening Point.* New York: A.A. Knopf, 1958. Reprint, Minneapolis: University of Minnesota Press, 1997.

———. *Runes of the North.* New York: A.A. Knopf, 1964. Reprint, Minneapolis: University of Minnesota Press, 1997.

———. *The Singing Wilderness.* New York: A.A. Knopf, 1956.

Paddock, Joe. *Keeper of the Wild: The Life of Ernest Oberholtzer.* St. Paul: Minnesota Historical Society Press, 2001.

Rutstrum, Calvin. *Once Upon a Wilderness.* New York: Macmillan, 1973.

Sutter, Barton. *Cold Comfort: Life at the Top of the Map.* Minneapolis: University of Minnesota Press, 1998.

Wood, Douglas. *Fawn Island.* Minneapolis: University of Minnesota Press, 2001.

———. "The Wildness Within." *Boundary Waters Journal* (Fall 1989). Reprint, *North Writers: A Strong Woods Collection.* Edited by John Henricksson. 1991.

About the Author

The author releasing a banded sharp-shinned hawk, Hawk Ridge, Duluth.

An avid Nordic ski racer, cyclist, sailor, canoeist and remarkably patient angler, Stephen Wilbers has taken sixty-four trips to the Boundary Waters Canoe Area Wilderness, as well as four trips to the wilds of Canada as a Boy Scout and one with his wife, Debbie, to Quetico Provincial Park. All told, he has spent about one year of his sixty-two years wilderness canoeing, and he hopes to make it two years before he dies.

His previously published books include *A Boundary Waters History: Canoeing Across Time* (also published by The History Press), a history of the Iowa Writers' Workshop, a chapbook of poems titled *This Northern Nonsense* about Ernest Oberholtzer (the gentle giant who helped save the Boundary Waters from development) and three books of writing instruction, including *Writing for Business* (winner of a Minnesota Book Award) and *Keys to Great Writing*.